WITNESS OF CHARITY

UNDERSTANDING THE TRUE MEANING
OF CHRISTIAN LOVE

J. F. RODRIGO

FOREWORD by BISHOP EMERITUS F. B. HENRY

WILLIAM T. McGRATTAN

BISHOP OF CALGARY

RESCRIPT

In accord with Canon 823 of the Code of canon Law, I hereby grant my permission to publish "WITNESS OF CHARITY — Understanding the true meaning of Christian love" by J.F. Rodrigo

It is my desire that you will use this work to spread the important message of true Christian charity that is so desperately needed in our world.

Notice of this rescript is to be printed on the reverse side of the title page of the book.

Given on the seventh day in the month of January in the year of our Lord two thousand twenty.

Sincerely in Christ,

Most Reverend William T. McGrattan,

Bishop of the Diocese of Calgary

ROMAN CATHOLIC DIOCESE OF CALGARY
Catholic Pastoral Centre | 120 17 Ave SW, Calgary, AB T2S 2T2
Phone: 403 218-5500 | www.calgarydiocese.ca

Witness of Charity

Understanding the True Meaning of Christian Love

2020
Trinity Project Publishing

Nihil Obstat: ✠ Most Reverend Frederick B. Henry
Bishop Emeritus of the Diocese of Calgary

Imprimatur: ✠ Most Reverend William T. McGrattan
Bishop of the Diocese of Calgary
January 7, 2020.

WITNESS of CHARITY: UNDERSTANDING THE TRUE MEANING of CHRISTIAN LOVE
Copyright © 2020, by TRINITY PROJECT PUBLISHING.

ISBN: 978-0-9959644-0-2

Holy Bible: All Scripture quotations are taken from the *New American Bible* (*NAB*) unless otherwise indicated. The text of the New American Bible With Revised New Testament Copyright © 1986, 1970 and the Revised Psalms of the New American Bible Copyright © 1991 Confraternity of Christian Doctrine, 3211 Fourth Street, N.E., Washington, DC 20017.

Catechism of the Catholic Church (*CCC*): All *CCC* quotations are taken from the Canadian Conference of Catholic Bishops popular and definitive edition first published in 2000. Copyright © Concacan Inc., 2000.

Catholic Encyclopedia: All *Catholic Encyclopedia* quotations are taken from the *Our Sunday Visitor's Catholic Encyclopedia* (Revised Edition). Copyright © Our Sunday Visitor, Inc., 1998.

Photo Credits:
Front Cover Image: "*Christ Crucified*" by Diego Velázquez, 1632; "*Jesus Washing Peter's Feet*" by Ford Madox Brown, c1852; "*The Good Samaritan*" by Dan Burr.

Cover and interior design by Blitsprint Inc. and TRINITY PROJECT PUBLISHING.

Published in Canada, by TRINITY PROJECT PUBLISHING.
Printed and bound in Canada.

To my niece and three nephews,
may you each be a witness of charity.

Contents

Abbreviations

OLD TESTAMENT

Genesis	Gen	1 Chronicles	1 Chron	Ecclesiastes	Eccl	Amos	Amos
Exodus	Ex	2 Chronicles	2 Chron	Song of Songs	Song	Obadiah	Obad
Leviticus	Lev	Ezra	Ezra	Wisdom	Wisdom	Jonah	Jonah
Numbers	Num	Nehemiah	Neh	Sirach	Sirach	Micah	Micah
Deuteronomy	Deut	Tobit	Tobit	Isaiah	Isa	Nahum	Nahum
Joshua	Josh	Judith	Jdth	Jeremiah	Jer	Habakkuk	Hab
Judges	Judg	Esther	Esth	Lamentations	Lam	Zephaniah	Zeph
Ruth	Ruth	1 Maccabees	1 Macc	Baruch	Baruch	Haggai	Hag
1 Samuel	1 Sam	2 Maccabees	2 Macc	Ezekiel	Ezek	Zechariah	Zech
2 Samuel	2 Sam	Job	Job	Daniel	Dan	Malachi	Mal
1 Kings	1 Kgs	Psalms	Ps	Hosea	Hosea		
2 Kings	2 Kgs	Proverbs	Prov	Joel	Joel		

NEW TESTAMENT

Matthew	Mt	2 Corinthians	2 Cor	1 Timothy	1 Tm	2 Peter	2 Pt
Mark	Mk	Galatians	Gal	2 Timothy	2 Tm	1 John	1 Jn
Luke	Lk	Ephesians	Eph	Titus	Ti	2 John	2 Jn
John	Jn	Philippians	Phil	Philemon	Phlm	3 John	3 Jn
Acts	Acts	Colossians	Col	Hebrews	Heb	Jude	Jude
Romans	Rom	1 Thessalonians	1 Thes	James	Jms	Revelation	Rv
1 Corinthians	1 Cor	2 Thessalonians	2 Thes	1 Peter	1 Pt		

OTHER

New American Bible	NAB
Catechism of the Catholic Church	CCC
Deus Caritas Est	DCE
Misericordiae Vultus	MV

Foreword

Experience teaches us that we sometimes need a gentle nudge or an elbow in ribs or a reminder to "lighten up," "pay attention," or "wake up."

In writing to the Philippians, Saint Paul exhorts some of his close friends:

> Therefore, my brothers and sisters, whom I love and long for, my joy and my crown, in this way stand firm in the Lord, beloved. I urge Euodia, and I urge Syntyche to come to a mutual understanding in the Lord. Yes, and I ask you also, my true companion, to help them, for they have struggled at my side in promoting the Gospel, along with Clement and my other co-workers, whose names are in the book of life. (Phil 4:1–3)

This little book, *Witness of Charity*, attempts to accomplish similar goals. It brings "fresh eyes" to some of our basic teachings on charity.

In our confused and troubled world, we mustn't allow ourselves to be lulled to sleep, to lose perspective, or be discouraged by the lack of clear thinking. A living relationship with Christ is decisive. We need to posit signs of hope. Charity is a theological virtue proper to those who abide in Christ, as a branch abides in the vine and bears much fruit.

✠ Bishop Emeritus F. B. Henry
Diocese of Calgary

Foreword

Preface

Always be ready
to give an answer to anyone
who asks you for a reason
for the hope that lies within you;
but do it with gentleness and compassion.

1 Peter 3:15

Not only am I a huge advocate of this directive, but also these words of Saint Peter have given me the motivation to embark on writing this book. This is unequivocally a firm directive to *all* Christians. To give a fuller understanding, let us look at the underlying Greek words. We are to

> ➤ *always*, ἀεί (aei/*ah-eye*), not occasionally, but constantly, at all times to
> ➤ *be ready*, ἕτοιμος (hetoimos/*het-oy'-mos*), that is to be prepared, equipped
> ➤ *to give an answer*, ἀπολογία (apologia/*ap-ol-og-ee'-ah*), an explanation, a logical defence, an articulation, to enlighten
> ➤ *anyone who asks you for a reason*, λόγος (logos/*log'-os*), literally a word, or a rational cause, an account, a teaching, a doctrine
> ➤ *for the hope*, ἐλπίς (elpis/*el-pece'*), the expectation, the confidence, the faith
> ➤ *that lies within you, but do it with gentleness*, πραΰτης (prautēs/*prah-oo'-tace*), mildness, meekness, modesty, humility
> ➤ *and compassion*, φόβος (phobos/*fob'-os*) or reverence, fear, and respectfulness (1 Pt 3:15).

This is not optional. I, therefore, hope and pray that this book gives us a clear and logical explanation of the fundamental teachings in the particular area of *Christian charity*, so, when required, we are prepared to articulate those specific principles on charity with humility and respect to all those who ask.

Because we are called to communicate our faith, I present this book as a study, in an explanatory, conversational style, or to be precise, a conversational *preaching* and *teaching* style. Consequently, *Witness of Charity: Understanding the True Meaning of Christian Love* is more of a kitchen table, "Bible on the one side, Catechism on the other side," contemplative, meditative, "let us struggle, grapple, and grow in our faith" type of read rather than a casual "curl up on the couch on a Sunday afternoon" read.

Keep in mind that the fundamentals of what we believe have a direct correlation to how we live. If our beliefs are sound, and we put them into practice, our life will inevitably be sound! If our beliefs are unsound, our life becomes unsound! Moreover, the frequent use of those faulty beliefs will continue to produce a faulty life. Unfortunately, as Christians, we profess a *belief* in Christ Jesus, but too many of us do not really understand *in* Whom (or even what) we believe, nor the *difference* that this belief we profess should make in our lives (*Note*[1]). Some of us are also caught up in private subjective revelations, in private religious practices, or even secular ideologies. These may seem right to us, "but the end of it leads to death" (Prov 14:12). We Christians are currently led to feel a false sense of security, causing us to be less alert, less aware, or less watchful. Well, it is time for us to *wake up* (Eph 5:14), be alert (1 Thes 5:6), truly understand the beliefs we profess, and live accordingly.

With this in mind and with this directive and conviction, I press forward in my *study* of God, so—through His grace—I may do what is asked of me. Interestingly, when writing about Truth (i.e., Jesus) or truths, some readers assume that the writer has *arrived* and is living the written reality. To be clear, that is not so with me. I have *not* arrived! As I preach and teach, a phenomenon happens: I find myself preaching and teaching mainly to myself. "I count myself one of the number of those who write as they learn and learn as they write," to use the words of Saint Augustine (*Note*[2]). You should also know that as the Lord is my witness, I struggle immensely with what I have written. I struggle with the truth that Christ Jesus presents to His Church. As I write, my own words convict me.

PREFACE

PUT ON THEN, AS God's CHOSEN ONES, holy and beloved,
HEARTFELT COMPASSION, kindness, lowliness, meekness, humility,
GENTLENESS, AND PATIENCE,
bEARING WITH ONE ANOTHER AND FORGIVING ONE ANOTHER,
if ONE HAS A GRIEVANCE OR complaint against another;
FORGIVING EACH OTHER; AS THE Lord HAS FORGIVEN YOU,
SO YOU ALSO MUST FORGIVE.
AND ABOVE ALL THESE PUT ON LOVE,
which binds EVERYTHING TOGETHER IN PERFECT HARMONY.
AND LET THE PEACE OF CHRIST CONTROL AND RULE IN YOUR HEARTS,
TO WHICH INDEED YOU WERE CALLED IN THE ONE body.
AND BE THANKFUL.
LET THE WORD OF CHRIST dwell IN YOU richly,
TEACH AND ADMONISH ONE ANOTHER IN ALL wisdom.
SINGING psalms, hymns, AND spiritual songs
WITH GRATITUDE AND THANKFULNESS IN YOUR HEARTS TO God.
AND WHATEVER YOU do, IN word OR IN deed,
do EVERYTHING IN THE NAME OF THE Lord JESUS,
GIVING THANKS TO God THE FATHER THROUGH Him.

Colossians 3:12-17[3]

A Note to the Reader

First, I have divided this study into chapters; the chapters, however, should *not* be read in isolation. An integration or synthesis exists within the chapters; I would like, therefore, to present this study as a continuous and unified thought.

Second, because *Witness of Charity: Understanding the True Meaning of Christian Love* is a *study*, I have started and ended it with a prayer (or Scripture passage). I hope it will guide our thoughts and set the necessary tone.

Third, I am using Endnotes in three different ways: (i) for basic citation, (ii) to define a theological word or term, and (iii) to give you additional information. For your ease, when used in this third way, I will state within parentheses the word (*Note*) with the reference number.

Fourth, in Appendix A, you will find my Methodology and Presuppositions. I recommend that you read this section before commencing the study (even though you might find it a little dry). However, if you do not see it as beneficial, feel free to skip it, or skim through it, and pick up whatever benefits you.

Finally, I would like to thank my family and friends who were kind enough to read and critique these studies in their original form. Your questions, concerns, comments, suggestions, objections, discussions, and encouragement have helped bring *Witness of Charity: Understanding the True Meaning of Christian Love* to this stage. Thank you!

Introduction

May the Lord increase you
and make you overflow with love for one another and for all.
May He strengthen your hearts, making them blameless and holy
before our God and Father at the coming of
our Lord Jesus the Christ with all His holy ones.

1 Thessalonians 3:12–13

When I think of what it means to be a witness of charity, three images of Christ come to mind.[4] As depicted on the cover, the first image, which I consider primary, is Jesus the Christ, crucified. The second is Jesus the Christ, washing His disciples' feet. The third image is Jesus the Christ, as the Good Samaritan.

As you read this study, I encourage you to bring these three images to mind. As we contemplate Christian charity, we will see interplay among these images that reveal a profound truth about charity. In these images, we not only see the true witness of charity, shown to us by none other than Christ Himself, but also we are confronted with the lived reality that we as Christians are called to imitate—to be the witness *of.* Yes, we are a witness *of*—not *to*—Charity, for we are not a witness *to* something or someone. We are a witness *of* Someone.

With that in mind, the focus of this study is for us to understand or to rediscover the true meaning of Christian charity, and then with that understanding, to live out that reality. I will, therefore, first concentrate on the fundamentals of charity, before focusing on its application (or how we are to live what we profess). It is unfortunate that most Christians are living a societal understanding of charity. In other words, Christians have integrated a non-Christian understanding of charity, and as a result, not only has *charity* lost its true Christian meaning, we have made this distortion our lived reality.

I realize that fundamentals may be somewhat technical. However, we must grasp them, so we may live them. As mentioned in the Preface, how we live and conduct our lives has a direct correlation to what we believe.

Cāritās is Christian love.
Therefore, it is a particular type of love,
which is rooted in *agape* (ἀγάπη).

Chapter 1 | Charity: The Christian Perspective

Charity, from the Latin word *cāritās*, is one of the three theological virtues[5] (the other two being faith and hope). If I were to ask the meaning of the word *charity*, most people would answer with one or a combination of the following: alms, donations to the poor, a generous action, or financial aid to the less fortunate (*Note*[6]). Although this is true, from a Christian point of view, charity not only means Christian works (corporal or spiritual works or acts) but also, on a deeper level, Christian *love*—moreover, a particular type of *love*.

So, what do I mean by "a particular type of love?" As Pope Benedict XVI puts it, what we have here is a "problem of language. Today, the term 'love' has become one of the most frequently used and misused words, a word to which we attach quite different meanings."[7] Pope Benedict XVI continues by saying that in today's culture, we have a

> vast semantic range of the word "love": we speak of love of country, love of one's profession, love between friends, love of work, love between parents and children, love between family members, love of neighbour and love of God.[8]
>
> | Pope Benedict XVI |

This is the problem we face. In the English language, we have only one word, *love*, to describe the different meanings or types of love mentioned above. In the Greek language, however, there are multiple words used for *love* (*Note*[9]). Within Scripture, three of these words are used (*Note*[10]). Here are the three Greek words found in the Bible:

1. ἀγάπη (agape/*agápā*)
2. ἔρως (eros/*érōs*)
3. φιλία (philia/*philia*)

Before we define these words, a word of caution—we should avoid two extremes. The first extreme is to compartmentalize love rigidly into these three words. The three different words are varied manifestations of the single reality—*love*. The other extreme is not to recognize that the single reality has individual meanings expressed in different words. Although these categories do not separate love in a general sense, they are yet distinctive.

Our goal is to be somewhere in between these two extremes. That is, we should recognize the beauty, the depth, and the individual nuances that enhance our understanding of the underlying meaning, reality, and varied manifestations of love in each of the Greek words for *love*. At the same time, we need to recognize that overlap and interplay exist among these three Greek words, which fundamentally reveal a single reality, for all three words ultimately mean *love*.

To love is to be vulnerable, and if we love properly, we will suffer. More can be said about love and suffering,[11] but for the moment, all we need to note is that despite this suffering and vulnerability, we, as humans, yearn to love and to be loved. This act of loving (giving love) and being loved (receiving love) takes on different realities. Here again, are the three Greek words conveying specific realities:

1) ἀγάπη (agape/*agápā*):

- **Sacrificial, self-sacrificing, unselfish, selfless love.**
- **Unconditional, unlimited, uncalculated, unmotivated, spontaneous love.**
- **Creative love.**
- **Covenant love.**
- **Downward movement from subject to object—"God's way to man."**

2) ἔρως (eros/érōs):

- Desire for the "beautiful and good."
- Passionate attraction love.
- The state of being "in love."
- Intimate, romantic love—but not always sexual in nature.
- Mystical love.
- Upward movement from subject to object — "man's way to God."

3) φιλία (philia/philía):

- Friendship, brotherhood, brotherly love.
- The acceptance of love—being open to receiving love.
- Has to do with the affection that results from interpersonal relationships and can also involve concern and care for another person.

Agape (ἀγάπη), "which occurs rather infrequently in Greek usage," Pope Benedict XVI writes, would nevertheless become the preferred word for love used by the New Testament writers.[12] A "new vision of love expressed through the word [agape (ἀγάπη)], clearly points to something new and distinct about the Christian understanding of love."[13] Here, we can see why, in the early Church, agape (ἀγάπη) also designated the meal that Christians celebrated together as an expression of Christ's sacrificial love for them, and, consequently, their love for each other. In this is agape (ἀγάπη): "not that we loved God, but He loved us" (1 Jn 4:10). It is a downward movement of love from God to us (Note[14]). Agape (ἀγάπη) starts with God's love for us. Through this agape (ἀγάπη), and by admitting God into our hearts, we are transformed, and we are able to love one another as God has loved us.

Eros (ἔρως) is used only twice in the Bible, in the Greek Old Testament, the Septuagint.[15] It is an outward movement of love for the "beautiful and good" in the other. Thus, *eros* (ἔρως) is also part of the outward upward movement of love from us toward the ultimate "Beautiful and Good." Most of us tend to equate *eros* (ἔρως) with sex, but this is not so. For one thing, sexual activity or experience can occur without love—without *eros* (ἔρως) or even without being in love. We should underscore that *eros* (ἔρως) is love. Therefore, in no way do we as Christians reject it, or say that there is a conflict between e*ros* (ἔρως) and *agape* (ἀγάπη) or *philia* (φιλία). Instead, we declare no to the twisted, destructive, and counterfeit forms of e*ros* (ἔρως)—referred to as "vulgar" *eros* (ἔρως), which strip us of our dignity and dehumanizes us.[16] When *eros* (ἔρως) is reduced to "sex," it becomes merely a commodity that can be bought and sold.[17] This is not love! This is not *eros* (ἔρως). Authentic *eros* (ἔρως), in the words of Pope Benedict XVI, "tends to rise 'in ecstasy' toward the Divine, to lead us beyond ourselves"[18] (*Note*[19]).

Philia (φιλία) "is used with an added depth of meaning in Saint John's Gospel in order to express the relationship between Jesus and His disciples."[20] An essential nuance of *philia* (φιλία) is that it is a love that is freely chosen, or moreover, the love that is open to receiving and accepting the love of another. Therefore, it is equated with the bride's love for her bridegroom. For example, we the Church as Bride, *philia* (φιλία) Christ Jesus our Bridegroom, by being open to Him and thus receiving His love.

To sum up, the Bible uses three different Greek words with particular meanings and different dimensions to convey a single reality—love. Again, we should not rigidly compartmentalize or completely separate these words, nor should we fail to recognize the specific meanings or nuances expressed by these three words. We should also note that the twisted states or tainted forms of these loves produce possessiveness, jealousy, covetousness, inordinate attachment, and the like. These perversions of love are *not* love in any of its forms, but a twisted state that we unfortunately sometimes call love.

Most of the material in this study comes from presentations I have given in the past at various parishes. In these presentations, I show the participants familiar scriptural passages that use the word *love* and then ask them to decipher the underlying Greek word. The participants enjoyed this exercise, even when they disagreed on the meaning of love in a particular Scripture passage. So, we shall mimic this reverse-translation exercise as we go through the following Scriptural passages. To do this effectively, try not to read ahead until you have done your translation.

Let us begin with 1 John 4:8: "God is love." What do you think? Which Greek word is used? If you said, "God is *agape* (ἀγάπη)" you would be correct! Yes, God is self-giving, unconditional, self-sacrificing love (*Note*[21]).

What about husbands' love for their wives? In his letter to the Ephesians, Saint Paul says, "Husbands, love your wives" (Eph 5:25). Moreover, he states, "Husbands should love their wives as their own body" (Eph 5:28). What Greek word for love is used here? Most husbands answer, *eros* (ἔρως). Well, to the surprise of most, in both cases the word used is *agape* (ἀγάπη): "Husbands, *agape* (ἀγάπη) your wives" (Eph 5:25), and "Husbands should *agape* (ἀγάπη) their wives as their own body" (Eph 5:28).

How about the flip side, namely, wives' love for their husbands? In his letter to Titus, Saint Paul tells women to "love their husbands" (Ti 2:4). What do you think? Is Saint Paul also asking wives to *agape* (ἀγάπη) their husbands? Interestingly, and to the surprise of most, he does not. He states, "Women are to *philia* (φιλία) their husbands" (Ti 2:4).

This book is not a study on marriage; and so, an in-depth analysis of the theological reasons that underlie this Scripture passage would be beyond the scope of this study. However, I would point out two things. First, a husband's love for his wife must mimic that of Christ's love for His Church (His bride). Just as "Christ loved [*agape* (ἀγάπη)] His Church and handed Himself over for Her" (Eph 5:25), a husband must *agape* (ἀγάπη) his wife and hand himself over for her (a self-giving sacrificial love). This understanding of love does not apply, however, in reverse, for a wife is not called to hand herself over for her husband in this way. On the contrary, she is called freely to choose him and, more importantly in that choice, be *open* to *allow* him to *agape* (ἀγάπη) her and to *receive* that *agape* (ἀγάπη) from him (*Note*[22]).

Second, stating, "husbands *agape* (ἀγάπη) your wives" (Eph 5:25) by no means excludes that a husband should *philia* (φιλία) his wife, for his wife, should be his best friend. Besides, by no means should he not *eros* (ἔρως) his wife, for his wife, should be the object of his desire, the passion of his life (*Note*[23]). This understanding also applies vice versa. By stating that wives "are to *philia* (φιλία) their husbands" (Ti 2:4) does not mean that a wife should not *eros* (ἔρως) or *agape* (ἀγάπη) her husband. Although the emphasis is on *agape* (ἀγάπη) for the husband, and *philia* (φιλία) for the wife—and the nuances each word brings—we must always remember that there is interplay among all of these Greek words.

Returning to the Scripture study, we will now look at a scene with which most of us are familiar: Saint Peter's threefold confession of love (*Note*[24]). The theological understanding and meanings behind the *threefold* confession are profound. For our study, however, we will focus only on the word *love*, for the underlying implications of the Greek word *love* give us additional insight into Jesus' dialogue with Peter.

Let us again start the translation exercise with Jesus' first question: "Simon, son of John, do you love me more than these?" (Jn 21:15). What do you think? Which one of these Greek words is Jesus using? If you translated *agape* (ἀγάπη), you would be correct! So, now we have Peter's answer: "Yes, Lord, you know that I love you" (Jn 21:15). Here we get our first insight by reading the Greek text, for Peter replies using the word *philia* (φιλία), not *agape* (ἀγάπη): "Yes, Lord, you know that I *philia* (φιλία) you" (Jn 21:15). Interesting?

To this *philia* (φιλία) response from Peter, Jesus asked the question a second time: "Simon, son of John, do you love me?" (Jn 21:16). Again, if you translated *agape* (ἀγάπη), you would be correct. To this, Peter's second reply is: "Yes, Lord, you know that I love you" (Jn 21:16). What do you think? Does Peter change his answer? Well, he does not. He replies with the word *philia* (φιλία).

Then, for the third and final time, Jesus asked Peter, "Simon, son of John, do you love me?" (Jn 21:17). We see here our second profound insight—Jesus changes the word He uses from *agape* (ἀγάπη) to *philia* (φιλία)—"Simon, son of John, do you *philia* (φιλία) me?" (Jn 21:17). To this third question, Peter answers: "Lord, you know everything; you know that I love you" (Jn 21:17). If you think by now Peter might have also changed the word for the love he uses, he does not; he again uses the word *philia* (φιλία).

From these two insights, there are three points I would like to make. First, this dialogue should give us a cause for hope. We might be just like Peter, unable totally to *agape* (ἀγάπη) Jesus at *this* moment in our life. We might say to Jesus, "Yes, I *philia* (φιλία) You" but for some reason "I cannot *agape* (ἀγάπη) You" (e.g., at this point in my life: I am not sure, I am not ready, or I do not have the strength). In this dialogue, Jesus is telling us that that is okay. Jesus even takes it a step further and comes down to Peter's level; by application, He comes down to our level to meet us where we are. Jesus does not force Peter, nor does He force us to declare something that we are unable to say. Rather, Jesus comforts Peter, and us, by changing the question to conform to our answer. He changes to meet us where *we are*, and then He patiently awaits our greater response.

This brings me to my second point, for here is the *key*, which applies to both points one and three. In our *philia* (φιλία) response, we must be willing to allow Jesus to work with us, through us, and in us, and most importantly *allow* Him to *agape* (ἀγάπη) us, and thus, through the power of the Holy Spirit, to change our *philia* (φιλία) response into self-giving, self-sacrificing *agape* (ἀγάπη) response (as He did with Peter on the day of Pentecost). Just because Jesus meets us where we are, we do not have a licence to remain where we are (Jn 8:10–11). We must allow Him to take us beyond that point.

The third point, on our part, we must follow Jesus' lead and meet other people where they are. However, we should not use this as a cop-out. Following Jesus' example means that we must also call others to something greater, something higher (*Note*[25]). We must call them to something that empowers them to reach their full potential. Yes, ultimately, we must call them to Christ Jesus.

Summarizing these three points, we can find comfort in Peter's answer, a comfort in where we are, and the realization of our calling to meet others where they are. However, we must also realize that we cannot remain where we are or use this as a cop-out when dealing with others. Remember, Jesus knows that within Peter's *philia* (φιλία) response, Peter is *open* and willing to allow Jesus to *agape* (ἀγάπη) him, and only in Jesus' *agape* (ἀγάπη) is he empowered to change his response to a reciprocal *agape* (ἀγάπη). Knowing this, Jesus continues to tell Peter:

> I say to you, when you were younger, you used to dress yourself and go where you wanted; but when you grow old, you will stretch out your hands, and someone else will dress you and lead you where you do not want to go. (Jn 21:18)

Yes, Jesus knows Peter would *agape* (ἀγάπη) Him. Jesus says these words to Peter knowing the kind of death that he would die to glorify God (Jn 21:19). "And when Jesus had said this, He said to him, 'Follow me'" (Jn 21:19). These words are not only for Peter; they also apply to you and me.

Continuing with our Scripture study, let us lastly look at, "You shall love your neighbour" (Mt 19:19, Mk 12:31, Lk 10:27, Rom 13:9, Gal 5:14, and Jms 2:8). So, is Jesus asking us to *agape* (ἀγάπη) our neighbour, or *eros* (ἔρως) our neighbour, or *philia* (φιλία) our neighbour? Well, in all the verses listed, written by different writers, the same word *agape* (ἀγάπη) is used. We must love our neighbour with self-giving, unconditional, self-sacrificial love. Knowing this, if you are now thinking it would be hard to *agape* (ἀγάπη) your neighbour, surprisingly, Jesus also uses the word *agape* (ἀγάπη) when He asks us to "love our enemies" (Mt 5:44 and Lk 6:35). During my presentations, this catches everyone off guard; some even ask, "How's this possible?"

In summary, from the multiple words in the Greek language describing the different meanings or types of love (i.e., our various lived realities of love) only three were used in the Bible—*agape* (ἀγάπη), *eros* (ἔρως), and *philia* (φιλία). From these three words, however, the lived reality expressed in Christian love is *agape* (ἀγάπη). Remember, when I said that *charity* means Christian *love*, and Christian love is "a particular type of love," well, I was alluding to *agape* (ἀγάπη). Charity is Christian love, and Christian love is *agape* (ἀγάπη); and thus, expressing it is a demanding task (*Note*[26]).

Unless otherwise stated, when I use the word *love* and when the word *love* is used within Church documents, homilies, and the like, it is *agape* (ἀγάπη) that is being used; for this is the underlying nuance of love or charity from a Christian point of view (*Note*[27]).

Agape (ἀγάπη) is willing the good of the other, for their sake.
Therefore, the supreme act of *agape* (ἀγάπη)
is to share Christ Jesus with others.

Chapter 2 | Charity: It is an Act of the "Will"

There is another aspect of the Christian love that goes beyond our cultural and societal understanding of love. Besides having a *problem of language*, we also have a *problem of definition*. Societally, love is mainly associated with emotion, feeling, impulse, affection, inclination, or sentiment. Christian love, *agape* (ἀγάπη), does not remove emotions and feelings from love but goes beyond them in a rational act of the will in obedience to the Truth (cf. 1 Tm 1:5). Emotions and feelings are notoriously unreliable and can be confusing or subjective. Sentiments come and go, and can be fleeting or relative. As Christians, we must act in the light of Truth, therefore moving from the subjective to the objective. In this process, our *will* must consequently be activated *by*, informed *by*, and conformed *to* the will of God.

Keeping in mind the definition of Christian love which we have already developed, *agape* (ἀγάπη) according to Saint Thomas Aquinas, is "to will the good [*bonum*] of another"[28] or "willing the good [*bonum*] of the other as other." We, as Christians, will the good of the other, not for our sake but for the sake of the other and the sake of Truth (Phil 2:4). As a result, we do not seek our rights, our advantage, or our way. No, we are not intellectually calculating our gain! For the good (*bonum*) of the other is not determined by what we can gain. The only consideration is the good of the other, not our personal interest, and no matter what our feelings might be towards the other. Christian love is a rational decision (*Note*[29]). We must decide to love the other "from a pure heart, a good conscience, and a sincere faith" (1 Tm 1:5b).

> Love . . . no longer is it self-seeking, a sinking in the intoxication of happiness; instead it seeks the good of the beloved: it becomes renunciation, and it is ready, and even willing, for sacrifice.[30]
>
> | Pope Benedict XVI |

In this decision, *agape* (ἀγάπη) is motivated by the need to see others succeed in life. The word *succeed* (or *success*) is not meant in a worldly sense. To succeed in life is to be *good*. Furthermore, Saint Thomas Aquinas[31] would say that being good, or helping others succeed in life, is to help them find the *Ultimate Good*, the *Highest Good*, the *Supreme Good*, the *Summum Bonum*—God Himself (*Note*[32]). Therefore, not only must this engagement of will and intellect align itself with God's will (as Pope Benedict XVI expressed, "God's will is no longer, for me, an alien will, something imposed on me from without by the commandments, but it is now my own will"[33]), we must also acknowledge that the *ultimate* act of love (*Note*[34]) is to bring others to God (*Note*[35]).

> Love is indeed "ecstasy," not in the sense of a moment of intoxication, but rather as a journey, an ongoing exodus out of the closed inward-looking self towards its liberation through self-giving, and thus towards authentic self-discovery and indeed the discovery of God.[36]
>
> | Pope Benedict XVI |

This is important and worth repeating: the definitive act of love, as a Christian, is to help others discover God. God is love, remember, *agape* (ἀγάπη), sacrificial, unconditional, self-giving love (cf. 1 Jn 4:8). God loves us, an encounter which also engages our will and intellect. When our will aligns itself with His will, we will want and desire to share His Truth and His love with others (e.g., family, friends, and acquaintances). Yes, this is the *ultimate* act of love—we must share the *Summum Bonum*, and thus help others discover God's love (*Note*[37]).

Some of you might question this statement by saying, "Doesn't Jesus say to us that the greatest act of love is 'to lay down one's life for one's friends'" (Jn 15:13)? So, how does this harmonize with the above statement of bringing a person to God? Here is how Saint Gregory the Great answers this question:

> The highest, the only proof of love, is to love our adversary . . . Our Lord came to die for His enemies,

but He says that He is going to lay down His life for His friends, to show us that by loving, we are able to gain over our enemies, so that they who persecute us are by anticipation our friends.[38]

| Saint Gregory the Great |

What would be the greatest *gain over our enemies* if not bringing them to God? What is the cross of Christ, the laying down of His life, if not a direct pointer to God? Doesn't the centurion witnessing this laying down of life say: "Truly this man was the Son of God" (Mk 15:39)? By laying down His life, doesn't Jesus bring His friends and His enemies to God? Even Saint Peter plainly states that the reason Christ died was that He might lead us to God (1 Pt 3:18). Therefore, aren't we called to do the same?

"Willing the good (*bonum*) of the other" is that; true *agape* (ἀγάπη), does *not* rejoice in the failures and mishaps of our neighbour or enemy. This is a subtle point. For example, when we gossip about our brother or sister, when we delight in their misfortune, when we find pleasure in their sin and affliction, when we have this inner happiness as hardship and difficulties come upon them, we find ourselves awfully far from willing their good (*Note[39]*).

Or, when we are envious and jealous of our brother or sister who is more talented than we are, who has a bigger house than we have, who has a stronger marriage than ours, who is better looking than we are, who has a superior job than we have, whose children are more gifted than ours, and so forth, we again find ourselves extremely far from *agape* (ἀγάπη) (*Note[40]*). So, beware!

All in all, to truly "love our neighbour" (and by extension, our enemy), we must go well beyond emotions, feelings, or sentiment. Love is a practical choice. Love is a rational choice. We must employ our will and truly "will the good of the other" in all aspects, for their sake. That is, we must help others to *succeed in life*, namely to be *good,* which means to find *the love of God in their lives*. Radical love is a service to Truth. Loving our neighbour, therefore, is not only about helping with the necessities of their temporal life, but it is for the most part about helping with their eternal life, namely, with their relationship with the True God.

CHARITY: IT IS AN ACT OF THE "Will"

To clarify, I am not saying that love should not have affections, emotions, and feelings (i.e., affectivity). Rather, Christian love, or charity, should go beyond affectivity to the realm of will. If not, how do we love a neighbour whom we dislike, or how do we love our enemy towards whom we might not have the kindest feelings? Wouldn't it be nonsense to suggest that we love our enemies with affectionate feelings? Pick an event from history you might consider to be evil. Think of the person, or persons, who perpetrated this evil. Let us assume that when you go to church this Sunday, the Mass intention was for that person. What would you do? Would you pray for that person? Would you pray for the soul of an Adolf Hitler, an Osama bin Laden, a Joseph Stalin, a Gadhafi, a Charles Manson, a Ted Bundy, or the like?

If your answer is "No," you are most likely saying no out of emotions and feelings you have for that person. As a Christian, however, we move beyond affectivity to use our will. For if you say "yes" to the above question, you understand that it is predominantly through the act of your will (and must not forget, through the grace of God) that you can say yes and pray for such a person.

To repeat, we are called to love our enemies and pray for those who persecute us (Mt 5:44 and Lk 6:35). We are called to "rejoice with those who rejoice, weep with those who weep" (Rom 12:15), to "have the same regard" for all (Rom 12:16), to "love one another with mutual affection" (Rom 12:10), to "hate what is evil" and to "hold on to what is good" (Rom 12:9), to "bless those who persecute" us (Rom 12:14), and not to repay "evil for evil" (Rom 12:17). Instead, if our "enemy is hungry, feed him; if he is thirsty, give him something to drink" (Rom 12:20).

This is the Gospel message. This is not just lip service. This must be a lived reality because it is the perfection of love. Christian *agape* (ἀγάπη) goes beyond natural love, and it is by doing this that we may be children of our Heavenly Father (Mt 5:43–45). Remember, if we *agape* (ἀγάπη) those who *agape* (ἀγάπη) us, this is not good enough (*Note*[41]): "For if you love those who love you, what recompense will you have?" (Mt 5:46). If we only greet and care for those whom we love and who love us, what is so remarkable about that (Mt 5:47)? Doesn't the non-Christian do the same (Mt 5:47)?

Christian *agape* (ἀγάπη) must go beyond the ordinary to the extraordinary (*Note*⁴²).

Before we move on, I would like to clarify one thing while we are on the topic of enemies. Some Christians have the misconception that to love our enemies (or for that matter our neighbours), we need to *like* them or *accept* their behaviour. This is *not* Christian teaching. Loving our enemies does not mean we have to like them. No! We need not be fond of them, and we need not like, condone, or accept their behaviour. If truth were told, we can despise what they do, hate what they stand for, even condemn, and correct the acts they have committed. Nevertheless, we must love them. God loves the sinner (i.e., us), but hates the sin, so we must also love the sinner, but hate the sin. That is, we must distinguish between the sinner and the sin. Even though we hate the *actions* of sinners, we must love them and, thus, always *will* their good and treat them accordingly—with their inherent God-given dignity. We need to reach out to them, care for them, challenge them, and admonish them to find good—eventually, the *Supreme Good* (*Summum Bonum*). We must "be of one mind, sympathetic, loving toward one another, compassionate, and humble, not return evil for evil, or insult for insult; but, on the contrary, a blessing, because to this we were called" (1 Pt 3:8–9).

Here is a simple example—parents love their children; however, they do not always agree with the decisions or actions of their child. Sometimes, the actions of a child can be entirely hurtful and painful. Still, the parents love them, always will their good, and treat them for their good. We must treat our enemies no differently.

If you think that *agape* (ἀγάπη) takes work, that it hurts, and that it moves us out of our comfort zone—you are correct! True *agape* (ἀγάπη) has to cost us. After reading this, if you think that true *agape* (ἀγάπη) is humanly impossible—i.e., "I can't do this?"—you are also correct. We recognize that our human efforts cannot achieve this *agape* (ἀγάπη). It is only through the grace of God that we, as Christians, can carry out this calling. Within this process, conversion or a self-transformation must take place within us, as stated by the Canadian Conference of Catholic Bishops:

> We need a deeper conversion of heart to take root . . .
> Without this conversion, there is no systematic

CHARITY: IT IS AN ACT OF THE "Will"

change. In the words of a popular song, all we need is love, but love as a pleasant and ephemeral feeling will not do. Real love requires a wrenching transformation, a letting go of self.[43]

| Canadian Conference of Catholic Bishops |

Another phenomenon occurs when we start with the premise of willing the good of the other rather than starting with our affectivity. By starting with willing the good of the other, our affectivity towards the other gradually changes positively. As we willingly *agape* (ἀγάπη) our neighbour and our enemy, our emotions and feelings towards our neighbour and our enemy are positively changed.

Shall we make this personal? Think of someone who has done ill or has been hostile to us. What are our emotions and feelings towards that person? Most likely they are of the negative variety. Our launching pad is that of resentment towards a person who harms us. As a result, our will might follow our affectivity and easily succumb to harming that person in return (directly or indirectly). Our reaction follows the negative emotions and feelings that surround this situation and becomes very difficult to change. Our negative emotions and feelings influence our will. Therefore, we might not only will harm to that person, but also we might want to hurt that person directly.

Now we will look at the same situation, the same person, with the starting premise of willing the good of that person. By reminding ourselves that, as a Christian, we are called to will the good of our neighbour and our enemy, we find it may positively influence our emotions and feelings towards them. In the words of C. S. Lewis:

> It would be quite wrong to think that the way to become charitable is to sit trying to manufacture affectionate feelings. Some people are "cold" by temperament; that may be a misfortune for them, but it is no more a sin than having a bad digestion is a sin; and it does not cut them out from the chance, or excuse them from the duty, of learning charity. The rule for all of us is perfectly simple. Do not waste

time bothering whether you "love" your neighbour; act as if you did. As soon as we do this we find one of the great secrets. When you are behaving as if you love someone, you will presently come to love him. If you injure someone you dislike, you will find yourself disliking him more. If you do him a good turn, you will find yourself disliking him less. There is, indeed, one exception. If you do him a good turn, not to please God and obey the law of charity, but to show him what a fine forgiving chap you are, and to put him in your debt, and then sit down to wait for his "gratitude," you will probably be disappointed. (People are not fools: they have a very quick eye for anything like showing off, or patronage). But whenever we do good to another self, just because it is a self, made (like us) by God, and desiring its own happiness as we desire ours, we shall have learned to love it a little more or, at least, to dislike it less.[44]

| C. S. Lewis |

We see this phenomenon played out in the lives of the Saints. Two examples that come to mind are Saint Francis and Saint Stephen. As the story goes:

Once while Saint Francis was singing praises to the Lord in French in a certain forest, thieves suddenly attacked him. When they savagely demanded who he was, the man of God answered confidently and forcefully, "I am the herald of the great King! What is it to you?" They beat him and threw him into a ditch filled with deep snow, saying, "Lie there, you stupid herald of God!" After they left, he rolled about to and fro, shook the snow off himself, and jumped out of the ditch. Exhilarated with great joy, he began in a loud voice to make the woods resound with praises to the Creator of all.[45]

| Thomas of Celano |

CHARITY: IT IS AN ACT OF THE "Will"

We know that Saint Stephen while being stoned to death did not ask for vengeance; he was not filled with hatred; he did not curse his murderers. On the contrary, he simply says out of love, "Lord, do not hold this sin against them" (Acts 7:60). These are the examples we must follow.

In sum, love—as in willing the good (*bonum*) of the other—is fundamental. If we do not have love, if we do not will the good of the other, we are nothing (1 Cor 13:2b). It is because we will the good of the other that we are patient with them, that we are kind towards them, that we are not jealous, pompous, nor rude to them (1 Cor 13:4). When we will the good of the other we are neither inflated, or quick-tempered nor do we brood over injury or seek our own interest (1 Cor 13:5). Willing the good of the other, means that we rejoice in truth and not in wrongdoing (1 Cor 13:6).

As many preachers have preached: love "bears all things," under any and all circumstances, yet it is not broken (1 Cor 13:7); love "believes all things," seeing the best of every person, yet it is undeceived (1 Cor 13:7); love "hopes all things," in all that comes its way, yet it is not put to shame (1 Cor 13:7); and love "endures all things," yet it is unweakened (1 Cor 13:7) (*Note*[46]).

Witness of Charity

Agape (ἀγάπη) is ethical and moral.
Therefore, the ends do not justify the means.

Chapter 3 | Charity: It is Ethical and Moral

The focus of this study is to rediscover the true meaning of Christian charity. Thus far, we have discussed the connection between charity and love. We have also talked about how a word such as love is used in different ways—for example, how love for ice cream, our dog, or our spouse differs.

Further, we have examined how secular influences have changed the meaning of the word love. As Christians, we have directly or indirectly, purposely or inadvertently, allowed the secular culture to influence our perspective on love. This influence has regrettably changed the original meaning of Christian love—*agape* (ἀγάπη). For example, when I ask the question, "What is the opposite of love?" the answer I receive from most Christians is "hate." As we now know, the reason behind this answer is the dominance of affectivity that society has assigned to love. However, as we also now know, from a Christian perspective, this does not hold, because the opposite of Christian love is selfishness, self-centredness, self-seeking, using, objectifying, or indifference—*not* hate. This secular influence, drawn to its conclusion, is that we do not love our neighbour as Jesus calls us to love our neighbour. In this concern, here are some questions to ponder: Can Hindus love their neighbour as Christians love their neighbour? Can Buddhists love their neighbour as Christians love their neighbour? Can Muslims love their neighbour as Christians love their neighbour? Can atheists love their neighbour as Christians love their neighbour?

Now, we also discussed that loving our neighbour is not only about taking care of their temporal needs, or for that matter, not only about taking care of their eternal needs. To truly love our neighbour, in a Christian sense, is to do both—as individually outlined and distinguished as the corporal works of mercy[47] (feed the hungry, give drink to the thirsty, clothe the naked, house the pilgrims, visit the sick, visit the imprisoned, and bury the dead), and the spiritual works of mercy[48] (advise those in doubt, teach the ignorant, admonish the sinners, console the afflicted, forgive offences, bear wrongs patiently, and pray for the living and the dead) (*Note*[49]). Dorothy Day, the cofounder of the Catholic Worker Movement, once said, "Everything a baptized person does each day should be directly or indirectly related to the corporal and spiritual works of mercy."[50] Only in doing both can we, as Christians, show authentic *agape* (ἀγάπη). Having said that, however, the focus thus far in this study has been on the eternal needs of our neighbour, for this is the greater of the two. The ultimate good we can do for our neighbours is to bring them to God. There is nothing more important than bringing people to God. Absolutely nothing!

In our quest to rediscover the true meaning of Christian love, or charity, we have laid a foundation upon which we can build. We can thus start looking at applications of Christian charity—which in a way, are also fundamental to its overall implications. So, let us continue, beginning with the very basics of ethics (*Note*[51]) and morality (*Note*[52]). We can call this Ethics and Morality 101 (*Note*[53]).

"When God created us, He made us subject to our own free choice" (Sirach 15:14); thus, we all have a God-given free will. This freedom makes us a "moral subject" (*CCC* #1749). As a result, even though we are not supposed to judge the person (Lk 6:37 and Mt 7:1–5), we can evaluate an act as a *good* act or an *evil* act (Jn 7:24, Mt 18:15–17, and 1 Cor 5:12–13). As the *Catechism of the Catholic Church* teaches us, "Human acts, can be morally evaluated . . . They are either good or evil" (*CCC* #1749).

Because of societal influences, Christians now often mistakenly refrain from judging or evaluating a moral act. We say, "Who are we to judge?" This statement only holds true when we are talking about *the person*; but when we are talking about *the act*, we are *called* to make a judgment on the act itself (Jn 7:24). There is nothing wrong with using our rationality to evaluate another person's actions. However, there is a difference between making a judgment on *the person* versus making a judgment on *the act* the person commits. The reason we do not judge *the person* is that we do not know that person's heart. We should always refrain from judging the person, for we are unaware of their inner intention or circumstances of their life. We are unaware of the environment, the trials, or the temptations that have shaped that person's being. Therefore, refraining from judging the person is not only the Christian thing to do, it is also a sensible thing to do.

Keep in mind that circumstances, although they provide an understanding of the reasons for the act, should not be used to excuse the act. Our sin is *ours*! Not only should the act itself be judged, but the person committing the act should therefore also be held responsible for such actions. We *can* judge the act, the sin, the human behaviour; we can also keep the individual accountable for the act, all the while letting *only* God be the judge of the state of that person's soul. I will come back to this point in Chapter 7, Charity and Mercy. For the moment, all we need to note is that the statement "Who are we to judge?" is not to be taken as a prohibition against the judgment of human behaviour or a ban on recognizing sin—it is to be taken as an admonition against *hypocrisy* (Mt 7:1–5), an admonition against *condemning* or judging *the person* (Lk 6:37). "Grant that we may never condemn or despise others, for we shall all one day face You as our judge," we pray.[54]

Moving along, most of us have heard this saying: "The road to hell is paved with good intentions." One interpretation of this saying is that we might intend to carry out a *good* act, but we do not follow through with it. Therefore, the *good* act remains merely an intention. Another interpretation and the one I will focus on is that our intentions are *good*, but our acts to get there are not so good (*Note*[55]). As Saint Thomas Aquinas states, "An evil action cannot be justified by reference to good intentions" (*CCC* #1759). That is to say, we "may not do evil so that good may result from it" (*CCC* #1756).

Every moral act depends on three things (*CCC* #1750):

1. The object (the "what" we do): this is the vehicle or any method used or chosen to achieve the intended outcome.
2. The intention (the "why" we do the act): this is not only the actual intended outcome or end result, but moreover the desires, the goal, or the "intention" of the acting subject concerning the intended outcome.
3. The circumstances (the "where," "when," and "how," etc.): these are the concrete conditions or situations in

which the act is performed or conditions or circumstances that contribute to the act (*Note*[56]).

For an act to be considered morally *good*, from a Christian perspective, it "requires the goodness of its object, of its intention, and of its circumstances together" (*CCC* #1760)—all three must be *good*. Some acts do not even pass the first stage, for the object itself is always wrong. For example, acts such as torture and rape are referred to as intrinsically evil acts, for they are always objectively wrong in and of themselves.

At the risk of oversimplification, let us use the terms *means* and *ends*, with which most of us are familiar. Here again, it is essential to remember that the ends do not justify the means. Our intentions of good (the ends) are not justified by using evil means of getting there (*CCC* #1759), and vice versa; "An evil end corrupts the action, even if the object is good in itself (such as praying and fasting 'in order to be seen by men')" (*CCC* #1755).

Although we have heard this many times, and it seems simple, Christians seldom apply this analysis, for it is more complicated than we think. Here are some examples. We work (means), so we may feed our family (good end), but what kind of job do we have? Does the job we have (means) propagate evil or good? We organize an event (means) to feed the poor (good end), but what are the means we use to achieve this end? Are the means (the event we organize, and the cost associated with it) good in and of themselves? Our intentions may be to protect our country and other countries from acts of terrorism (good ends), but how are we doing that? Are the means we use to protect our country also good? So, do you now see how this works? By the way, the saying, "By any means necessary," is not Christian.

As Christians, this is just the start of the questions we need to ask concerning every aspect of the life decisions we make. Yes, the congruency of the object, the intention, and the circumstances concerning the morality of a human action is more problematic than we think; likewise, deciphering the goodness of each component can also be taxing.

To demonstrate this, here is an exercise. Use the above application and analyze these specific contentious issues. Should a

Christian nurse, working in an operating theatre of a well-renowned medical facility, give a scalpel to a doctor performing an abortion? Should a Christian software programmer, working for a cutting edge software company, create code for an illicit program? Should a Christian couple who have a deep love for children but are unable to conceive, use any means at their disposal (medical or otherwise) to have children? Should a Christian son or daughter, out of concern for their elderly terminally ill and suffering parents, euthanize them? Should a Christian, suffering from a debilitating illness, request doctor-assisted suicide? Should Christian parents who know about their child's lesbian or gay tendencies advocate and condone same-sex marriages?

This is your exercise. I will not give you answers to these life questions, for that is not the purpose of this study (*Note*[57]). My goal is to provide a foundational understanding rooted in Christian principles of love and Truth, which can help us *inform our conscience* to answer these questions in a fruitful Christian manner within our daily Christian journey; thus, the goal is to do what God is asking us to do, and not make life decision based on our own desires.

Besides, although I have not discussed it here, the progression from morality or moral works to established habit or *virtue* also applies here. What I have stated in this chapter has more to do with the application of morality or, we can say, the technical aspect of morality and moral decision-making. However, we do not want to remain in the realm of moral decision-making—we want to move into the realm of living *virtuous lives,* which by default means we are making truly moral decisions.

Yes, *agape* (ἀγάπη) is virtuous! It is ethical and moral. Thus, we cannot love without being ethical and moral.

What we do is not as important as why we do it.
Therefore, what we do must always be rooted in
Why we do it.

Chapter 4 | Charity and Its Order

The *impetus* of true Christian love can only proceed from Christ's *agape* (ἀγάπη). Christ, therefore, must be the *centre* of everything we do. We are not secular humanists (*Note*[58]). That is, as a Christian, we should not ascribe to any variation of secular humanism.

We are not social workers or aid workers. We are literally *slaves* of Christ (Col 3:24 and Phil 1:1) and therefore must be grounded in Christ. For those reasons, we recognize that not only in Christ *can* we do the things we do, but also *only* in Christ *must* we do the things we do.

To understand the foundations, context, and characteristics of authentic Christian charity, we needed to define and examine the bonds linking charity with love and with works. Having accomplished the first step (the link between charity and love), it is now time to illustrate how charity and love link with works.

Begin with another Scripture study. I want to compare and contrast Saint Paul's letter to the Romans, in which Saint Paul seems to argue that Abraham was justified by faith, with that of the letter of Saint James, in which Saint James seems to argue that works justified Abraham. Let us begin by carefully reading Saint Paul's letter to the Romans:

> [If] Abraham was justified on the basis of his works, he has reason to boast; but this was not so in the sight of God. For what does the Scripture say? "Abraham believed God, and it was credited to him as righteousness." A worker's wage is credited not as a gift, but as something due. But when one does not work, yet believes in the one who justifies the ungodly, his faith is credited as righteousness. So also, David declares the blessedness of the person to whom God credits righteousness apart from works. (Rom 4:2–6)

Now we will compare this with the letter of Saint James:

What good is it, my brothers, if someone says he has faith but does not have works? Can that faith save him? If a brother or sister has nothing to wear and has no food for the day, and one of you says to them, "Go in peace, keep warm, and eat well," but you do not give them the necessities of the body, what good is it? So also faith of itself, if it does not have works, is dead. Indeed someone might say, "You have faith and I have works." (Jms 2:14–18a)

Do you want proof, you ignoramus, that faith without works is useless? Was not Abraham our father justified by works when he offered his son Isaac upon the altar? (Jms 2:20–21)

At first glance, this may seem like a contradiction. So, are Saint Paul and Saint James contradicting each other? No, of course not. Faith and works are meant to be held together, not to be reduced to one or the other (*Note*[59]). *Faith* and *hope* are synonymous, and *works* and *love* are also synonymous. Therefore, Saint James continues by stating that Abraham's

faith was active along with his works, and faith was completed by the works. Thus, the Scripture was fulfilled that says, "Abraham believed God, and it was credited to him as righteousness," and he was called "the friend of God." See how a person is justified by works and not by faith alone . . . For just as a body without a spirit is dead, so also faith without works is dead. (Jms 2:22–24 and 2:26)

Our works are a demonstration of our faith in living action (Eph 2:10). Alternatively, we might even say that our works are the fruit of our faith (cf. Mt 7:16). In Christ, the only thing that counts is faith working, expressing itself, and energizing itself through His love (Gal 5:6). Thus, held together, we can easily conclude that Saint Paul and Saint James are in concert.

Here we now see the order *to* charity. Our charity must always start with our faith—in Christ. In Christ, our faith must be active along with our works, and therefore, our faith finds completion by our works (Jms 2:22).

Keeping this in mind, let us elaborate. Picture this: a Christian and an atheist are volunteering at their local soup kitchen. They are both behind the counter serving the homeless population within their city. As the homeless line up and walk by them, each smiles, greets, and serves accordingly. You and I are standing in the corner of the room watching this unfold. I turn to you and ask you, "What is the difference between this Christian and this atheist who are volunteering in this soup kitchen?"

I have used this illustration in my group presentations. Most participants answer by saying there is *no* difference between the two individuals, that they are both helping people; they are both helping the poor; they are both helping the marginalized in society. Even though the latter part of this comment is correct, that they are both helping people, the former part of the answer is somewhat problematic, for there *must* be a fundamental difference between the Christian and the atheist in this example.

As said, we as Christians are not humanists, nor are we merely social workers or aid workers. We are not a charity (as in a charitable organization) or an NGO (non-government organization) or some not-for-profit organization. No, absolutely not! We are Christians. It is therefore understood, that we must *always be* in Christ, to be a true witness of Christ, and we must be able to receive His love, to be able to spread His love.

All our plans and works are futile and empty if not rooted in His love, in Him. As the psalmist declares: "If the Lord does not build the house, in vain do its builders labour . . . In vain is your earlier rising, your going later to rest" (Ps 127:1-2). In vain are all our works—in vain is all our love—if not purified and rooted in Him. We are not mere workers, we are His workers—we are a witness of Him.

Therefore, the difference between the Christian and the atheist in the above example is that the atheist is serving the homeless based on a humanistic worldview. The Christian, however, must be grounded in Christ and therefore is serving the homeless in Christ, with Christ, through Christ, and in Christ's *agape* (ἀγάπη). The Christian must be the face of Christ in that soup kitchen, and the

CHARITY AND ITS ORDER

Christian must *see* the face of Christ in the face of those being served. Broadening the scope, here is how Saint Teresa of Calcutta puts it:

> The Jesus who becomes bread to satisfy our hunger also becomes that naked person, that homeless and lonely and unwanted person, that leper or drunkard or drug addict or prostitute, so that we can satisfy His hunger to be loved by us through the love we show them.[60]
>
> | Saint Teresa of Calcutta |

Now some may argue that there are some atheists who are more *Christian* than some Christians are. If you agree with this or a similar statement, you are *not* getting the point. Even though we could unequivocally state that it is better to be an atheist than to be a Christian whose actions are not centred in Christ (or a nominal Christian); to say that they are *more* Christian or a *better* Christian is plainly wrong. Putting aside the fact that this statement is illogical on many different levels, simply put, atheists cannot be better "Christians," no matter how many *good* works or acts they perform. Why? Why couldn't an atheist be a better Christian? First, works, per se, do not qualify us to be Christians. Second, the inner disposition (the *impetus*) is more important than *any* outward works. Third, and most importantly, being a Christian is an *identity* based on a covenant-relationship with a Person. It is not based on following any set of rules, or any outward works, or any acts performed (as we will see in Chapter 5, Charity and the Law).

To be clear, the point I am making is that the act a person performs is not as important as the underlying impetus, for it is the impetus—our relationship with Christ— that gives meaning to the act. "Practical activity will always be insufficient, unless it visibly expresses a love for man, a love nourished by an encounter with Christ," Pope Benedict XVI wrote in his encyclical.[61]

Again, there is an order *to* charity. Our encounter with Christ must nourish us, and only then will our practical activity be sufficient. I like to put it this way: the *what* we do as a Christian must always be rooted in the *Why* we do it—and the *Why* we do something must at all times go before the *what* that we are doing. We do *what* we do because of Christ and in Christ (the *Why*); therefore, in a way, it does not matter what we do—for if we are *truly* acting in Christ, then we are doing what is genuinely Christian, what is truly moral, what is truly virtuous, and what is truly *agape* (ἀγάπη)—there is no separation or distinction (*Note*[62]).

To use a term from theologians, this order is also connected to *right worship*. If we mess up our worship or our order to charity, we begin worshipping things other than God (e.g., wealth, power, pleasure, and our own desires, wants, pride, egos, and even humanity itself); then the *what* we do, or the *secondary cause*, can become supreme (*Note*[63]). We can also start to *worship* our *good* deeds. If I may use an extreme example using the pro-life movement, in which we see some pro-lifers blow-up abortion clinics or kill doctors who perform abortions. Not only are the means of *what* they do wrong; *what* they do is no longer grounded in Christ for it now becomes rooted in their own ideology.

Ponder the words of Jean-Baptiste Chautard: "There are many apostolic workers who never do anything purely for [Christ]. In all things, they seek themselves, and they are always secretly mingling their own interests with the glory of God."[64] Doing what is "right" is not good enough. We might do what is right for the wrong reason or motive. We must therefore vigilantly watch for hidden purposes, ideologies, and self-interests (cf. Phil 2:3); and, always remember the order *to* charity.

Grappling with this is good. We need to ask: "Am I one of those apostolic workers?" So, let us take this a step forward and apply this rationale to our own works. Here are some questions that we should reflect upon: Are the charitable works I perform a witness of Christ or are they a witness to my own desires, my own wants, my own goals, my own ego, or myself? Do I give in secret (Mt 6:2), or do I give with trumpets blasting? Do I give without my left hand knowing what my right hand is doing (Mt 6:3), or do I give to receive, with an expectation of recognition and reward, or with a deep self-seeking interest?

For, if our works, as Christians, are not centred in Christ, they will inevitably be centred on our own desires, wants, ideology, personal philosophy, or self-interest, thus fulfilling nothing other than our own ego, vanity, and pride. It does not matter how many "good" works we perform and what our peers think of them. The works in themselves are *meaningless* if they are not done in Christ. Granted, it may be meaningful in the eyes of the world, but not in the eyes of Christ. The doing of "good" works is not good enough.

Remember, Jesus' *works* while walking this earth were always secondary to His *identity* (Who do you say that I am?—Mt 16:15, Mk 8:29, and Lk 9:20) and His *impetus* (His Father's will—Jn 8:28 and 12:48–49). The works He did were always the will of the Father. Our works are also secondary to our *identity* (Christian) and our *impetus* (Christ), and our works must always be the will of Christ. Only in Christ do our works have meaning.

It is therefore mandatory for us to begin at the feet of Christ in prayer and ask *Him* to *infuse* our works and deeds (*Note*[65]). We may be the greatest orator, we may be able to sing in angelic tongues, we may be able to cure the sick and heal the wounded, we may have given away everything we owned and taken a vow of poverty, we may be the greatest theologian with an in-depth knowledge and understanding of Sacred Scripture; but if anything and everything we do is not grounded in Christ, in Truth, in charity, in love, and in His works, this is all meaningless, worthless, useless, and empty (1 Cor 13:1–3).

In the words of Thomas A. Kempis:

> True charity is not self-seeking, it goes all the way for the honour and glory of God. Those who are charitable envy no one, nor do they seek their own pleasure, but desire above all things to find their joy in God . . . Whatever is done out of true charity, no matter how small and insignificant, is profitable in the eyes of God.[66]
>
> | Thomas A. Kempis |

Continuing, we will now build upon this understanding. However, due to this being somewhat technical, I thought it would be best to recap systematically what we have learned thus far, using a chart as a visual aid:

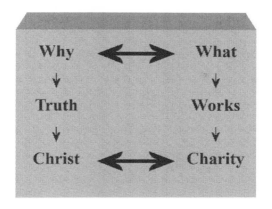

As we can see, on the one hand, we have a linear pattern. We can also consider the left column as the first part of the commandment: "You shall love the Lord, your God, with all your heart, with all your being, with all your strength, and with all your mind" (Lk 10:27), and the right column as the second part of the commandment: "and your neighbour as yourself" (Lk 10:27).

On the other hand, we have a circular pattern. The elements of the diagram are connected. Keep in mind, the first column must always go before the second column (namely, the *Why* must always go before the *what* or *Truth* must always go before *works*), and the second column must always be in the first column (namely, the *what* must always be in the *Why* or *works* must always be in *Truth*). That said, all these terms are also connected and somewhat inter-changeable.

As a result, the title of this study could have also easily been *Witness of Love* or *Witness of Works*. Because Truth and charity are also inseparable, the title of this study could have also been *Witness of Truth* or even more accurately, *Witness of Christ*.

Yes, a true witness of charity is a witness of *Christ*! What else can they be? The Saints understood this. They did not compart-mentalize charity. They absorbed and internalized the understanding that a true witness of charity should fundamentally be, and only be, a witness of *Christ* Himself.

When love means God's love revealed in Christ, given to us without reference to our merits, then love to neighbour is inevitable, almost self-evident; it is the outflow of the Divine love man has received, seeking its way through Him to others. We need not, indeed cannot, point to anything else but God's love as the reason for our love to our neighbour. It is "unmotivated" like God's love with which it is given, of which it is an extension. If a motivation can be found, it is purely causal, inasmuch as love to one's neighbour springs by inner necessity put of the experience of Divine love.[67]

| Anders Nygren |

Our love must flow from His love. Let me emphasize this point again by stressing the importance of being attached to Christ Himself as opposed to being attached to "good acts." We are called to carry out our mission in Him—in Truth. This mission does not change based on popular opinion nor by passing fads. For without Christ—without Truth—our love is reduced to mere sentimentality.

Now, if all this holds true, you might have concluded by now that Hindus, Buddhists, Muslims, atheists, or any non-Christian, cannot love their neighbours as Christians love their neighbours. If so, you are correct. This conclusion is not an insult (*Note*[68]). It is a reality.

If you are grappling with this conclusion, let me go over it once more in three steps.

Step One: in the Old Testament (in the Book of Leviticus), the Lord speaks to Moses and tells him, "You shall love your neighbour as yourself" (Lev 19:18b). In this Old Testament context, the word "neighbour" was interpreted and thus relegated only to the Israelite community (Lev 19:18a).

Step Two: in the New Testament, when the scribe and scholar of the law tested Jesus by questioning Him concerning the commandments, Jesus proposes two principal commandments: love of God and love of neighbour (*Note*[69]). During these discussions concerning the latter (the love of neighbour), Jesus repeats the command from Leviticus, "You shall love your neighbour as yourself" (Mt 22:39, Mt

19:19, Mk 12:31, 12:33, and Lk 10:27) (*Note*[70]). However, unlike the context of the Old Testament, Jesus clarifies (i.e., emphasizes the original intended meaning), and thus extends or give its proper meaning to encompass every human being, even enemies (Lk 10:29ff). Also in the New Testament, we receive what we now refer to as the Golden Rule: "Do to others whatever you would have them do to you" (Mt 7:12 and Lk 6:31). In a manner of speaking, these statements were given in a *general* way (first to a particular community, then to every human person). However, it does not stop here. Concerning His disciples, Jesus takes it a step further.

Step Three: here Jesus gives *us*, His *disciples*, something stricter, something literally bound to Himself, a *new* commandment, which is to, "Love one another as I have loved you" (Jn 13:34 and Jn 15:12). Yes, this is a new commandment to the Christian community, and it is attached to Jesus Himself. Our understanding of love is not society's understanding, but it is His understanding of love. Our love is of one mind and heart with His love. Our calling is to love our neighbour as *He* loves—not as Krishna loves, not as Buddha loves, not as Mohammed loves—we are called to love as Christ loves. As a result, a Christian's *agape* (ἀγάπη) is fundamentally different, for it is rooted in Christ's *agape* (ἀγάπη), in His very Person, in the love of God Himself. This *is* our identification (Jn 13:35).

If we think about it, not to recognize this point would be an insult and offensive to all non-Christians. For, would it not be offensive, on our part, to tell atheists that they must love as Jesus loves? Or to a Buddhist, that they must see the image of Jesus in their neighbour? Or, would it not be insulting to tell any non-Christian that the love they share for their neighbour is the love of Christ?

Keep in mind that I am stating this in an *objective* sense and not in a *subjective* sense; therefore Christian *agape* (ἀγάπη) differs in both nature and expression when objectively compared to that (love) of a non-Christian. To be clear, it is critical to mention that this applies only to *agape* (ἀγάπη), as we have defined it, and thus does *not* apply to *eros* (ἔρως) love, nor *philia* (φιλία) love, given or shown by a Hindu, Buddhist, Muslim, atheist, or any non-Christian (*Note*[71]).

Once this is understood, as alluded, this brings up another issue. For if all this holds true, if we know that *Truth*, with a capital *T* is objective, *the Truth*, which is Christ Himself (Jn 14:6), we must also conclude that Christian *love* is also objective. To this, I also say, yes!

A Christian's love must be rooted in Christ: "Love one another as *I* have loved you" (Jn 13:34; *emphasis* added). Consequently, as Hans Urs von Balthasar has affirmed, human holiness is objectively "identifiable and discernible." We can also claim *agape* (ἀγάπη) is also objectively *identifiable and discernible*: "This is *how all will know* that you are my disciples, if you have *love* for one another" (Jn 13:35, *emphasis* added; also cf. Lk 6:44). Ask yourself, if our definition of *love* doesn't differ from that of a non-Christian, how would anyone know we are His disciples?

Think about it! Saint Paul states that if he does not have love, he is nothing (1 Cor 13:2). Saint Polycarp says, "Anyone who has love is far from sin."[72] Saint Augustine tells us we can "love and do whatever we wish" (*Note*[73]). Now, if love isn't defined the way we have described it here, if love isn't objective and rooted in Christ but is subjective to the unpredictability of the person, are these statements not ludicrous? If *love* is defined only in terms of affectivity, can these statements be made? Of course not! It would be subject to each person's whims, feelings, emotions, and desires, wouldn't it? We can therefore unequivocally state that for Saint Paul, Saint Polycarp, and Saint Augustine, love, true *agape* (ἀγάπη), is rooted in objective Truth, which is Christ. It is only in the objectivity of love that these statements can be made.

If we love with Christ's love and in Christ's love, not only is our love objectively discernible, we also cannot sin; for *true* Christian charity, true *agape* (ἀγάπη) cannot sin. Sin, as Saint Catherine of Siena puts it, is the defective understanding of Truth. This defective understanding of Truth leads to a defective understanding of love, a defective understanding of the love of God, a defective understanding of the love of neighbour, and a defective understanding of the love of self (*Note*[74]). Our defective understanding of love, within the Christian community, stems from a defective understanding of Truth.

Do not fool yourself into thinking that we can love in some other way other than in Truth (cf. Eph 4:15) (*Note*[75]).

> Love without truth is sentimentality; it supports and affirms us but keeps us in denial about our flaws.

Truth without love is harshness; it gives us information but in such a way that we cannot really hear it.[76]

| Timothy Keller |

Our societal emphasis on political correctness (defined as: "conforming to a particular sociopolitical ideology or point of view, concerned with avoiding offence"[77]) is not *agape* (ἀγάπη). Our society's *twisted* form of tolerance, compassion, inclusivity, rights, and equality are also not congruent with *agape* (ἀγάπη). Alternatively, forcing Truth down someone's throat is not *agape* (ἀγάπη). Do not be carried about by human trickery and deceit (cf. Eph 4:14). For, we cannot love someone without being in the Truth and sharing the Truth, which is Christ Himself (*Note*[78]). Do not be afraid to speak Truth in love, without ambiguity (*Note*[79]). Our lives should express Truth in all things—we must talk in Truth, deal in Truth, and live in Truth—all in love (cf. Eph 4:15).

———

In the introduction of Benedict XVI's last encyclical, *Caritas in Veritate* (Charity in Truth), he gives us an excellent summary of the main points that we have discussed. This is a rich text packed with meaning, so I would encourage you to read carefully and unpack what Pope Benedict XVI is telling us:

Charity in truth, to which Jesus Christ bore witness by His earthly life and especially by His death and resurrection, is the principal driving force behind the authentic development of every person and of all humanity. Love—*caritas*—is an extraordinary force which leads people to opt for courageous and generous engagement in the field of justice and peace. It is a force that has its origin in God, Eternal Love and Absolute Truth. Each person finds his good by adherence to God's plan for him, in order to realize it fully: in this plan, he finds his truth, and

CHARITY AND ITS ORDER

through adherence to this truth he becomes free (cf. Jn 8:22).

To defend the truth, to articulate it with humility and conviction, and to bear witness to it in life are therefore exacting and indispensable forms of charity. Charity, in fact, "rejoices in the truth" (1 Cor 13:6). All people feel the interior impulse to love authentically: love and truth never abandon them completely, because these are the vocation planted by God in the heart and mind of every human person. The search for love and truth is purified and liberated by Jesus Christ from the impoverishment that our humanity brings to it, and He reveals to us in all its fullness the initiative of love and the plan for true life that God has prepared for us. In Christ, *charity in truth* becomes the Face of His Person, a vocation for us to love our brothers and sisters in the truth of His plan. Indeed, He Himself is the Truth (cf. Jn 14:6).[80]

| Pope Benedict XVI |

To summarize Pope Benedict XVI, *agape* (ἀγάπη) has its *origins in God, Eternal Love*, and *Absolute Truth*. In that Truth, we are set *free*, for we find our *good* in God's plan and His will for us. Stating this Truth, and living this truth, is the form of charity that we, as Christians, are called to—this is our vocation.

Let us end this chapter by listening to the same message, given in the profound yet simple words of Saint Teresa of Calcutta (*Note*[81]):

For our vocation is *not* to serve the poor—your vocation is *not* to take care of the sick in the hospitals, or to teach. Our vocation is to belong to Jesus, with the conviction that nothing and nobody will separate us from the love of Christ; and that is why we need a complete surrender in obedience. The Church has given us this gift to belong to God; it has accepted us, accepted our consecration, accepted our lives. So this is something that we can understand only when we realize, what is our vocation? And, the work we have been entrusted, the work of our obedience, of our surrender, is our love for Jesus, in the living action. And, this is where you and I, must be able to face Jesus, and to surrender to Him completely. Because if we realize that we belong to Jesus, naturally He has a right to use us.[82]

| Saint Teresa of Calcutta |

The law is rooted in His *agape* (ἀγάπη).
Therefore, love is the decipherer of the law.

Chapter 5 | Charity and the Law

Let us begin this chapter by first defining the word law. For,

> there are four important references intended by the
> word "*law*" when used in the New Testament: (i) all
> commandments and stipulations which God gave to
> Moses (also known as the Mosaic law); (ii) the
> historical as well as juridical material in the
> Pentateuch [the first five books of the Bible]; (iii) all
> of the Old Testament, which can collectively be
> regarded as "law" [which also includes moral and
> liturgical law]; and, (iv) the oral traditions embodying
> the teachings of great rabbinical figures (*Note*[83]).
>
> | *Catholic Encyclopedia* |

Although it is typical to view what I am about to say as a
reference to the Ten Commandments (or in the broader sense, the
Mosaic law), neither the Old Testament nor the New Testament
always distinguishes these four references. In fact, all four references,
as noted above, are intertwined; for every aspect of Israelite life, was
directed towards God.[84]

The law stands as a whole. We can classify it into various
references or categories for teaching purposes, but the law is one.
Because of that, I shall also refer to all four references simply as the
"*law*."

With this understanding, and based on what has been said thus
far, let me ask a question: do you think that the *law* applies to us?
Well, it might come as a shock to most (especially when we think of
the Ten Commandments) that in a manner speaking, the *law* and its
legal claims do not apply to us. Some reading this might even be
ready to scream "heresy"! If so, I am willing to scream "paradox"!
Yes, what we have is a paradox.

We know that Jesus did *not* come to abolish the law (Mt 5:17).
We also know "it is easier for heaven and earth to pass away than for
the smallest part of a letter of the law to become invalid" (Lk 16:17

and Mt 5:18). On the other hand, however, in Jesus and "through His flesh," He *does* abolish "the law with its commandments and legal claims" (Eph 2:14–15). In Jesus, the law ends (Rom 10:4) (*Note*[85]). Therefore the law is *not* abolished, but at the same time, it *is* abolished in Him (Mt 5:17 and Eph 2:15). This is the paradox.

In this paradox, "we are [now] invited to rediscover [the law] in the Person of our Master who is its perfect fulfillment" (*CCC* #2053).

> Jesus fulfills these [four] definitions of *law*, and thus surpasses it (Mt 5:17–20), because Jesus is the way to God. The *"law"*—as a reference to Old Testament as a whole—is comprehensive, revelatory, permanently valuable and consists of an intrinsic and indissoluble amalgam of moral, liturgical and juridical guidelines . . . [However] the Gospel announces the Christo-centric fulfillment of law, pointing out that contact with God is not by means of physical circumcision (Rom 2:28; 3:1; Gal 2:3; 7; 5:6) or observance of traditional applications of the Mosaic law (Gal 2:16; 3:2; 5:10; Rom 2:15; 3:20; 28).
>
> So, while the law is holy and good (Rom 7:12; 16), an expression of God's will (Rom 2:27), and it does teach, it does not have the power to make holy, to transform, to renew.
>
> | *Catholic Encyclopedia* |

In Jesus the Christ, our Master, the law is now fulfilled—in its totality—in *His* Person: "Do not think that I have come to abolish the law or the prophets, I have come not to abolish but to fulfill" (Mt 5:17).

In this Scripture passage, Saint Matthew uses the Greek word πληρόω (plēroō/play-ro'-o), which is translated into English as *fulfill*. This Greek word has two dominant meanings. The first definition of *plēroō* (πληρόω) has an eschatological[86] sense, and the second definition is to complete, carry out through to the end, render perfect, bring to pass, ratify, or accomplish. In this chapter we will focus on the first definition; we will study the second definition later in Chapter 7, Charity and Mercy.

By using the first definition of *plēroō* (πληρόω), we receive a *key* found in all of the New Testament writers, which is that Christ Jesus is the lens through Whom the entire Old Testament Scriptures are to be interpreted. Therefore, the entire Old Testament Scriptures literally find their *fulfillment* in the Person of Jesus, including the *entire* law. "For Christ is the end of the law" (Rom 10:4a).

To grasp this fully, we will now unpack this in two separate steps. In the first step, we need to *understand* the law, now *in* Christ Jesus; and in the second step, we need to *interpret* the law, again, *in* Christ Jesus. We shall start with this new *understanding* of the law, in Christ.

———————————

Saint Paul, writing to his Jewish brothers and sisters in Rome who were well acquainted with the law, makes his argument concerning this new understanding of the law, in Christ:

> Are you unaware, brothers and sisters, that the law has jurisdiction over one as long as one lives? Thus, a married woman is bound by law to her living husband; but if her husband dies, she is released from the law in respect to her husband. Consequently, while her husband is alive she will be called an adulteress if she consorts with another man. But if her husband dies she is free from that law, and she is not an adulteress if she consorts with another man.
>
> In the same way, my brothers and sisters, you also were put to death to the law through the body of Christ, so that you might belong to another, to the One who was raised from the dead in order that we might bear fruit for God. For when we were in the flesh, our sinful passions, awakened by the law, worked in our members to bear fruit for death. But now we are released from the law, dead to what held

us captive, so that we may serve in the newness of the spirit and not under the obsolete letter. (Rom 7:1–6)

After this comment, Saint Paul anticipates that some of his readers might assume or conclude that the law is somehow sinful in itself. To this conclusion, he clearly states that it is not (Rom 7:7–12). What Saint Paul is arguing, however, is that we now have a different understanding of the law because of Christ Jesus. He explains this by demonstrating how the law binds only the living, not the dead. The example he gives is marriage, which binds a couple in life, but not after either one of them dies.

The same principle applies to us. Through our baptism, we have literally died to our old self, have been buried with Christ (Rom 6:3), and have risen to new life with Him (Col 2:11-12). Now that we are joined to Christ, we are dead to sin (Rom 6:2) and free from the law (Rom 7:6). As a result, Saint Paul concludes his argument by emphatically stating:

> Now there is no condemnation for those who are in Christ Jesus. For the law of the Spirit of life in Christ Jesus has freed you from the law of sin and death. For what the law, weakened by the flesh, was powerless to do, this God has done: by sending His own Son in the likeness of sinful flesh and for the sake of sin, He condemned sin in the flesh, so that the righteous decree of the law might be fulfilled in us, who live not according to the flesh but according to the Spirit.
> For those who live according to the flesh are concerned with the things of the flesh, but those who live according to the Spirit with the things of the Spirit. The concern of the flesh is death, but the concern of the Spirit is life and peace. For the concern of the flesh is hostility toward God; it does not submit to the law of God, nor can it; and those who are in the flesh cannot please God. But you are not in the flesh; on the contrary, you are in the Spirit, if only the Spirit of God dwells in you.

Whoever does not have the Spirit of Christ does not belong to Him. But if Christ is in you, although the body is dead because of sin, the Spirit is alive because of righteousness. If the Spirit of the One who raised Jesus from the dead dwells in you, the One who raised Christ from the dead will give life to your mortal bodies also, through His Spirit that dwells in you. Consequently, brothers and sisters, we are not debtors to the flesh, to live according to the flesh. For if you live according to the flesh, you will die, but if by the Spirit you put to death the deeds of the body, you will live. (Rom 8:1–13)

As we can see, Saint Paul methodically unpacks this new understanding of the law in Christ Jesus. Things have now changed. What the law could not do, Christ accomplished through His redemptive work (cf. Acts 13:3 and Acts 15:5–11). Now that we are baptized in Christ and have died with Him, we participate in His accomplishment. Therefore,

let no one, then, pass judgment on you in matters of food and drink or with regard to a festival or new moon or Sabbath. These are shadows of things to come; the reality belongs to Christ. Let no one disqualify you, delighting in self-abasement and worship of angels, taking his stand on visions, inflated without reason by his fleshly mind, and not holding closely to the head, from whom the whole body, supported and held together by its ligaments and bonds, achieves the growth that comes from God. If you died with Christ to the elemental powers of the world, why do you submit to regulations as if you were still living in the world? "Do not handle! Do not taste! Do not touch!" These are all things destined to perish with use; they accord with human precepts and teachings. While they have a semblance of wisdom in rigour of devotion and self-abasement and severity to

CHARITY AND THE LAW

the body, they are of no value against gratification of the flesh. (Col 2:16–23)

Amazing! We no longer need the old for the new has come (Col 2:20). Although well intended, the teachings of the past—"Do not handle! Do not taste! Do not touch!"—do not apply to us anymore in the new (Col 2:21). There it is, the original *understanding* of the law, in Christ.

To summarize, the law has no jurisdiction over us (Rom 7:1), for in Christ we are freed from the law (*Note*[87]) and its condemnation (Rom 8:1–2), the old has passed, and we are made anew in Him (Gal 4:4–7); therefore, we must now live this new reality (Col 2:20).

This now brings us to the second step: how are we to *interpret* the law in Christ? Simply put, the entire law is derived from and summed up in these two commandments:

> You shall love the Lord, your God, with all your heart, with all your soul, and with all your mind, [for] this is the greatest and the first commandment [this comes from Deut 6:5; also cf. 30:6]; [and] the second is like it: You shall love your neighbour as yourself [this comes from Lev 19:18]. (Mt 22:37–39; also cf. Mk 12:30–31 and Lk 10:27)

Why is this so? Why, from all the commandments (eventually numbered to be 613 in total), does Jesus distil the law to these two? It is because in these two commandments the entirety of the Law and the Prophets (i.e., the Old Testament) are encompassed (Mt 22:40):

> The commandments, "You shall not commit adultery; you shall not kill; you shall not steal; you shall not covet," and whatever other commandment there may be, are summed up in this saying, "You shall love your neighbour as yourself." Love does no evil to the neighbour; hence, love is the fulfillment of the law. (Rom 13:9–10)

WITNESS of CHARITY

Again, amazing! If we love the Lord our God with all our heart, with all our soul, and with all our mind (in other words, with the *totality* of our being), and if we love our neighbour as ourselves (in Truth), we, in a manner of speaking, do not need the law (Gal 5:22–23; also cf. Gal 5:1) (*Note*[88]); for, if we love in Truth, we *will not*, or *cannot* break the law or go against the teaching of the prophets, i.e., the fulfillment of the law (Rom 13:10).

Additionally, let us not miss an important point. That is, the proper object of *agape* (ἀγάπη) is God Himself, and God Himself teaches us how we should *agape* (ἀγάπη) (cf. Jer 31:33). Here is a simple example that might help. The law states: "You shall not commit adultery" (Ex 20:14). However, the law does not tell you to love your spouse. God teaches you to love your spouse. Listening to God, if you genuinely love your spouse, in Truth (cf. Eph 5:21-33), would you commit adultery? Of course not! Even the thought of it would not cross your mind. But here is the thing, it is the "in Truth" part that comes first. We must first strive and start with our love of God.

> Consequently it is not the wife who shall teach the husband how he should love her, or the husband his wife, or a friend his friend, or associates their associates, but it is God who shall teach every individual how he or she should love.[89]
>
> | Søren Kierkegaard |

Christian *agape* (ἀγάπη) therefore is incapable of sinning, and it is incapable of breaking God's commandments because it starts with our love for God Himself. Our love of neighbour *rests* upon our love of God, and it is, therefore, impossible to break the *law*. If we are living the law of *Truth*, the law of the *Lord*, the law of *charity*, doesn't the *law* itself become *mute* (Gal 5:18)? "For in Christ Jesus, neither circumcision nor uncircumcision [i.e., the *law*] counts for anything, but only faith working through love" (Gal 5:6).

All we need to do is *agape* (ἀγάπη) the Lord our God, and in Him and through Him and with Him (that is, in a faith that is infused and energized by Him), we *agape* (ἀγάπη) one another, for in that love we fulfill the law. Keep in mind these two laws are interlocked,

CHARITY AND THE LAW

they cannot be separated; nevertheless, they are distinctly two. As a Christian, we cannot love our neighbour (horizontal) without the love of God (vertical), and we cannot love God without loving our neighbour (1 Jn 4:20). However, the horizontal (love of neighbour) must always have the vertical (love of God) as its foundation.

Based on this interpretation, this realization of the law, Saint Augustine can proclaim, "Love, and do whatever we wish."[90] Saint Paul can unequivocally tell us, "Owe nothing to anyone, except to love one another; for the one who loves another has fulfilled the law" (Rom 13:8; also cf. Rom 13:10 and Gal 5:14). And Saint Bernard, abbot and Doctor of the Church, can affirm,

> Love is sufficient of itself; it gives pleasure by itself and because of itself. It is its own merit, its own reward, love looks for no cause outside itself, no effect beyond itself. Its profit lies in its practise. I love because I love; I love that I may love.[91]
>
> | Saint Bernard |

To recap *interpreting* the law in Christ: love of God and love of neighbour summarizes the entire law (Mt 22:40); love thus fulfills the law and in no way opposes or contradicts the law (Rom 13:10 and Gal 5:13). Therefore if we *agape* (ἀγάπη) in Truth, we do not need the law (Gal 5:22–23).

─────────

To be clear, I am not saying we should throw out the law (Mt 5:18). The commandments are fundamental; they are God's law (Deut 11:1 and Josh 22:5). The law not only gives us knowledge of sin (Rom 5:13), they can be used to discern God's will, help us train in righteousness, and thus, help us conform our will to that of God's (cf. 2 Tm 3:16–17). Our lives as Christians should not oppose or contradict the law (*Note*[92]). However, what I am saying is that we are called to have a deeper understanding (cf. Heb 7:12), and a complete interpretation of the law now in Christ, in *agape* (ἀγάπη).

Let me state this from another perspective, for we basically only have two choices. In our first choice: we can keep the works of the law by our own strength, and thus live by doing and depend on the law for our salvation (Gal 3:12). However, Saint Paul calls this choice a *curse*, for "Cursed be everyone who does not persevere in doing all the things written in the book of the law" (Gal 3:10)—yes, *all* things! Saint Paul, therefore so rightly concludes, "that no one is justified before God by the law" (Gal 3:11; also cf. Ps 143:2). Why? Because we all fall short—yes, we are unable to keep the law by our own strength. For that reason, God in His *agape* (ἀγάπη) sent His only Son, born of a woman, born under the law, to deliver from the law of those who were subject to it (Gal 4:4-5a).

What does this mean? It means that God's *agape* (ἀγάπη) for us is primary; it is not based on anything of our doing. Even the law itself cannot contain God's *agape* (ἀγάπη) for us. So, God sent His only Son in the likeness of sinful flesh as the sin offering, thereby condemning sin in the flesh so that the just demands of the law be fulfilled in us who live, not according to the flesh, but according to the Spirit (Rom 8:3-4). It is in this *agape* (ἀγάπη) of God we receive our second choice: we can now live by faith, and in faith, *depend* on Jesus for our salvation (Gal 3:11). Here we understand, that "the law does not depend on faith" (Gal 3:12) and the law was put in place as a guardian, to teach and guide us (Gal 3:24). But now in Jesus, we are guided by the Spirit in faith, thus no longer in need of the law as a guardian (Gal 5:18). Let me repeat, now that faith has come we are no longer under a guardian or disciplinarian (i.e., the law); for through faith, we are all children of God in Jesus (Gal 3:25–26).

Now, if we pick the latter, then we live in the Spirit in faith, let us therefore also follow the Spirit in faith (Gal 5:25). What does that mean? Well, "the fruit of the Spirit is love, joy, peace, patience, kindness, generosity, faithfulness, gentleness, self-control" (Gal 5:22), so our lives should demonstrate and live by these fruits. Our faith cannot remain dormant (Jms 2:14); for "faith of itself, if it does not have works, is dead" (Jms 2:17). We "who were baptized into Christ have clothed ourselves with Christ" (Gal 3:27; also cf. Gal 5:24); therefore we must live that reality.

So in essence, we are brought back to the law in a circular pattern. The starting point is the *law*. Because Christ is the fulfillment of the law, we move to a new *understanding* of the law (in Christ). With this, we are now called to move to a new *interpretation* of the

CHARITY AND THE LAW

law (in Christ)—to a radically deeper, intensified, internalized meaning and reality of the law (*Note*[93]). Thus, we embrace the entire law, but this time in Christ.

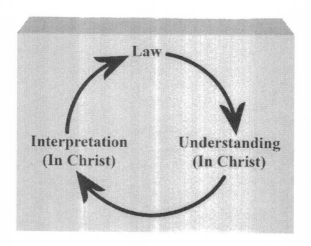

Yes, we approach the law again, from its intended perspective—in Him, in His *agape* (ἀγάπη) (Jn 13:34-35, 15:12, and 15:17)—remembering that He is the fulfillment. With this perspective, we not only realize that the law was rooted in His *agape* (ἀγάπη), we know that the law *is* His *agape* (ἀγάπη). Yes, the *law* is love! This is the new standard of the law for us Christians.

Here now is the realization. As we come to this new standard of the law, the *new* law—which Saint Paul calls the *law of Christ* (1 Cor 9:21 and Gal 6:2), and Saint James calls the *law of freedom* (Jms 1:25 and 2:12), and the *royal law*, literally the *kingly law* (Jms 2:8), or as we are calling it here, the *law of love* (*Note*[94])—we realize that it is impossible to live out this law through our own strength (for examples see Mt 5:21–22 and 5:27–28). Although we may argue that this also holds true concerning the law itself, there however was a subtle implication—by the wording "thou shall not"—that it was somehow up to us, or possible for us to carry out the law through our own strength (cf. Lk 18:20-21). With the law of love, that implication is no longer there (*Note*[95]). The focus changes from us (self-engaged) to God (God-engaged). For we can now clearly see that the law of

WITNESS of CHARITY

love shows us the true meaning of the law and that it can *only* be accomplished through God's empowerment in our lives.

To explain this further, we shall turn to the Gospel of Saint Matthew. First, Jesus tells us,

> Amen, I say to you, until heaven and earth pass away, not the smallest letter or the smallest part of a letter will pass from the law, until all things have taken place. Therefore, whoever breaks one of the least of these commandments and teaches others to do so will be called least in the Kingdom of Heaven. But whoever obeys and teaches these commandments will be called greatest in the Kingdom of Heaven. (Mt 5:17–19)

He continues by saying, "I tell you, unless your righteousness surpasses that of the scribes and Pharisees, you will not enter into the Kingdom of Heaven" (Mt 5:20). This statement must have caught the disciples off guard. How's this even possible, they might have thought? Remember, the Pharisees even tithed their mint, dill, cumin, and rue (Mt 23:23 and Lk 11:42). They were meticulous in their keeping of the law, so how was it possible to surpass them? Well, we get the answer to this from Jesus Himself:

> You have heard that it was said to your ancestors, "You shall not kill; and whoever kills will be liable to judgment." But I say to you, whoever is angry with his brother will be liable to judgment, and whoever says to his brother, "Raqa," [worthless imbecile] will be answerable to the Sanhedrin, and whoever says, "You fool," will be liable to fiery Gehenna. Therefore, if you bring your gift to the altar, and there recall that your brother has anything against you, leave your gift there at the altar, go first and be reconciled with your brother, and then come and offer your gift. (Mt 5:21–24)
> You have heard that it was said, "You shall not commit adultery." But I say to you, everyone who

looks at a woman with lust has already committed adultery with her in his heart. (Mt 5:27-28)
You have heard that it was said, "An eye for an eye and a tooth for a tooth." But I say to you, offer no resistance to one who is evil. When someone strikes you on your right cheek, turn the other one to him as well. (Mt 5:38–39)
You have heard that it was said, "You shall love your neighbour and hate your enemy." But I say to you, love your enemies, and pray for those who persecute you. (Mt 5:43–44)

In Jesus' answer, we see the original intention of the law and thus demands of the law of love. This is how we must surpass the scribes and Pharisees. It is so demanding that we might even say it is impossible. Just like the disciples, we might cry out "Who then can be saved?" (Mt 19:25). To this, Jesus answers, for humans "this is impossible, but for God all things are possible" (Mt 19:26). Yes, Jesus gives us the *ability* and infuses us with the *grace* (*Note*[96]) to make this impossible task possible. He will not ask us to carry out the law of love without giving us the means. Remember He fulfills the law, and all we have to do is participate in His fulfillment. This is not an abdication of our responsibility; on the contrary, it is a realization that we are in a joint venture with God. For only in Him, with Him, and through Him can we accomplish this new standard of the law, this law of love; as Pope Benedict XVI puts it, "Being a Christian is not the result of an ethical choice or a lofty idea [i.e., being a good person or keeping the law—self-engaged], but the encounter with an event, a Person [God-engaged] which gives life a new horizon and a decisive direction."[97] This is the realization.

While we are on the subject, there are two last points I would like to make. First, we may argue that Jesus cannot be suggesting that the act of lusting after someone, showing anger, or hatred toward someone is akin to the actual act of committing adultery or murdering someone. If this is our argument, we are essentially missing the point. The argument is moot. Why? Because Jesus is clearly stating that the mere avoidance of committing an act of adultery or murdering a person (which is the external act the scribes and Pharisees focused on) is just not good enough, for we must not even think the thought. Our thoughts and inner disposition are of great consequence; it should not go against the law of love, which was the original intention of the commandments. Jesus is correcting the inadequacy of the interpretations and giving us the real meaning of the law and the commandments. Namely, that we should also pay attention to our inner motives and disposition, for a harmony (congruence) must exist between what we do and what is in our heart, which is at the root of the law of love. Our encounter with Jesus must change us and impel us to go beyond the mere avoidance of any particular act to understanding the inner disposition that we are called to have. This is the new standard. This is the law of love that we are called to exemplify, which can only be accomplished through Christ Jesus.

My last point is this. Now that we are "guided by the Holy Spirit" and not "under the law" (Gal 5:18), we must move away from a sense of fear or obligation. That is, we must do what we do, not because of some sort of legal edict, or from mere duty, or because we are caught up in some kind of distorted legalism, or out of fear of punishment. No! We must come to that stage at which we do what we do purely out of *agape* (ἀγάπη) for Him, and in that love, we find our *joy* and *fulfillment*.

> [We] must do [monetarily or otherwise] as already determined, without [fear], sadness, or compulsion, for God loves a cheerful giver. Moreover, God is able to make every grace abundant for you, so that in all things, always having all you need, you may have an abundance for every good work. (2 Cor 9:7–8)

We must keep God's law because we *love* Him, we *thirst* for Him, we find *joy* in Him, and we *desire* to do His will, not because we are duty-bound or out of fear, but because we have a love for Him which is so deep that we do not want to offend Him, disappoint Him, or hurt Him. Even though the "law is holy, and the commandments are holy and righteous and good" (Rom 7:12), we no longer need

CHARITY AND THE LAW

stone tablets to guide us (Jer 31:33), for doing His will should be our *joy* and *delight* (Ps 40:9).

Love is "the pursuit of our own joy in the Holy joy of the Beloved," John Piper wrote.[98] It goes beyond keeping a mere set of rules, to a movement of reciprocating His love— in a joyful reaction.

Let me give a small example that might help. A teenage daughter has a curfew. Through the law of her parents, she returns home at a specific preset time. The parents' hope is this—that the teenager is not coming home because she is forced to or because she fears punishment. They hope she is returning home because she knows her parents love her and are concerned for her well-being. And in knowing that parental love, she responds to that love *in kind* by following the set curfew (for keeping the curfew has now become an expression of her reciprocal love). Yes, it is no longer a parental *law* that must be followed; it is a mutual and reciprocating act of love. This is the perfection in *agape* (ἀγάπη). For, there is no obligation in love (Sirach 15:14–15), nor is there fear in love; but perfect *agape* (ἀγάπη) is in freedom, and it "drives out fear, because fear has to do with punishment, and so one who fears [or feels obligated] is not yet perfect in love" (1 Jn 4:18).

Let us end this chapter and bridge ourselves to the next, with a reflection from Saint Gregory the Great:

> How must we interpret this law of God? How, if not by love? Listen to Truth speaking of this law: *This is my commandment, that you love one another.* Listen to Paul: *The whole law,* he declares, *is summed up in love;* and again: *Help one another in your troubles, and you will fulfill the law of Christ.* The law of Christ—does anything other than love more fittingly describe it? Truly we are keeping this law when, out of love, we go to the help of a brother in trouble.
>
> Love's lively concern for others is reflected in all the virtues. It begins with two commands, but it soon embraces many more. Paul gives a good summary of

its various aspects. *Love is patient,* he says, *and kind; it is never jealous or conceited; its conduct is blameless; it is not ambitious, not selfish, not quick to take offence; it harbours no evil thoughts, does not gloat over other people's sins, but is gladdened by an upright life.*

The man ruled by this love shows his *patience* by bearing wrongs with equanimity; his *kindness* by generously repaying good for evil. Jealousy is foreign to him. It is impossible to envy worldly success when he has no worldly desires. He is not *conceited.*

The prizes he covets lie within; outward blessings do not elate him. His conduct is *blameless,* for he cannot do wrong in devoting himself entirely to the love of God and his neighbour. He is not *ambitious.* The welfare of his own soul is what he cares about. Apart from that he seeks nothing.

He is not *selfish.* Unable to keep anything he has in this world, he is as indifferent to it as if it were another's. Indeed, in his eyes nothing is his own. He is *not quick to take offence.* Even under provocation, thought of revenge never crosses his mind. The reward he seeks hereafter will be greater in proportion to his endurance.

He harbours *no evil thoughts.* Hatred is utterly rooted out of a heart whose only love is goodness. Thoughts that defile a man can find no entry. He *does not gloat over* other people's *sins.* No, an enemy's fall affords him no delight, for loving all men, he longs for their salvation.

On the other hand, *he is gladdened by an upright life.* Since he loves others as himself, he takes as much pleasure in whatever good he sees in them as if the progress were his own.[99]

| Saint Gregory the Great |

CHARITY AND THE LAW

The Good Samaritan is more than a model to follow;
it is a way of life.
Therefore, we must go and do likewise.

CHApter 6 | CHARity ANd the Good SAMARiTAN Model

The Good Samaritan parable has a few different theological interpretations. Here, I first present the parable as a *model* (given to us by Christ). Then I will argue that emulating this model is *not* enough, for a Christian must go beyond this being a mere model, to a *lifestyle*.

In other words, there are two parts: first, the presentation of the Good Samaritan parable as *the* model of helping our neighbour in a time of need; and second, the realization that as a Christian, this help is still inadequate and insufficient, for the help we give our neighbour must be rooted in Christ (i.e., we must be Christ to our neighbour). And as a result, the model should not remain just a model; it must become a *way of life*.

Two cautionary notes. First, you may think this section contradicts what I have said so far. Well, this is not the case. Although our focus on Christian love has primarily been on the eternal needs of our neighbours, their temporal needs are just as essential (Jms 2:15–16). As stated, we are called to do both.

Remember Dorothy Day's statement: "Everything a baptized person does each day should be directly or indirectly related to the corporal and spiritual works of mercy."[100] Therefore, in this chapter the focus shifts from the spiritual (or eternal) needs of our neighbours to their corporal (or temporal) needs. For both must be held in concert.

Second, to avoid any misunderstandings (and to be crystal-clear), I affirm that in no way am I denouncing charitable giving via a charitable organization (*Note*[101]), nor am I denouncing volunteering, nor am I saying that good cannot come from either action.

I am, however, saying that Christians are called to go beyond *mere* volunteering or donating. Thus, the focus here is on that personal, tactile, one-on-one encounter which is at the crux of being a Christian—this is the Christian ideal.

The primary or ideal method of Christian giving (or love), as taught by Christ, is subtle, for it is rooted in the daily life of a Christian. This inner attitude or disposition is demonstrated to us in the Good Samaritan parable. If you are not familiar with it, you might want to read it before you continue (Lk 10:30–37).

This parable—or as I am now calling it, the Good Samaritan *model*—is *not* about going out and doing something (e.g., volunteering), nor is it about fulfilling an obligation of charitable giving (e.g., donating a percentage of your income). The Good Samaritan model fundamentally moves us beyond that to a natural and joy-filled way of daily living. Without neglecting to volunteer or donating, we are called to be that Good Samaritan and joyfully *agape* (ἀγάπη) our neighbour (cf. Mt 23:23).

Listen. Using modern terms, the Samaritan traveller could have very easily taken his cell phone, called up one of the leading charitable organizations, and donated. But he did not. He could have very quickly set up a "fund-raising campaign" and raised funds for this victim. But he did not. No, the Samaritan traveller knelt beside the victim, cleaned his wounds, bandaged them, then picked him up, placed him in his vehicle, took him to the nearest care clinic, and took care of him (cf. Lk 10:34). Not only did the Samaritan support the victim monetarily (cf. Lk 10:35), he supported him out of a real act of love and mercy, as his neighbour (cf. Lk 10:36–37). Now, here is the core teaching, Jesus tells us, just as He said to the scholar of the law, "Go and do likewise" (Lk 10:37).

We need not look for some cause to which to give our time, talent, or money. Helping our neighbour who is in need is not something abstract; it is not something we must go out and do as if it were part of a day's work, for our *neighbour* is that person who is immediately and directly in front of us. The Good Samaritan model is about being attentive and responsive to the immediate needs of *that* neighbour (who could be our father, mother, brother, sister, spouse, friend, stranger, *or* enemy). Yes, the opportunity literally comes to us in our daily living; unlike the priest or Levite (Lk 10:31–32), we must be open to that cause, to that opportunity and, in *all* humility, help our neighbour in *that* time of need.

The model of the Good Samaritan requires us to go out and get our hands dirty (literally). This is not only a personal, one-on-one encounter with the poor, the marginalized, and the outcasts of society; it is also, as pointed out, a personal one-on-one encounter with the person standing next to us, where we touch them and *agape* (ἀγάπη) them. This is a tactile operation (cf. Mt 8:3 and Lk 5:13), it is not just a sterile dispensation of monetary funds. If we say we love God, we must show it. We need to stop talking about it (the love we have for God) and live it. Going to church and hearing the Word is good, but not good enough; we must put the living Word we hear into living action (Jms 1:22). We must prove it! The proof we *agape* (ἀγάπη) God and that we are not mere listeners of His Word is found in our *agape* (ἀγάπη) of our neighbour.

Why? When we neglect or hurt our neighbour, we are neglecting and hurting Jesus Himself. Conversely, when we *agape* (ἀγάπη) our neighbour in their temporal needs, we love Christ Jesus (Mt 25:40). For when we care for our neighbour, we are actually caring for Christ's body. He tells us:

> I was hungry and you gave me food, I was thirsty and you gave me to drink, a stranger and you welcomed me, naked and you clothed me, ill and you cared for me. (Mt 25:35–36)

Therefore, knowing this must call us to a joyful disposition. Our *agape* (ἀγάπη) for Christ must motivate our *agape* (ἀγάπη) of our neighbour (*Note*[102]). For our encounter with our neighbour *is* an encounter with Christ. In our neighbour, we *touch* Christ Himself. So, rejoice (cf. Phil 4:4–5)!

Just as we do not seek Christ as much as He seeks us, we do not seek this encounter as much as the encounter seeks us. The Good Samaritan model is a way of life in which we, as Christians, are open to God's changing our plans anytime, anywhere, as He so wishes. Therefore, the *key* is this: when faced with this encounter, we must be open to the will of God not only by making ourselves available to this encounter but also by being open to changing our plans.

This is a matter of who is in charge of our lives. Are we in charge of our lives? Do we want to write our own ticket? Or do we want God to be the writer of our lives? Do we let God be in charge of our lives? Are we willing to be open to the inconvenience of our neighbour? Are we ready to make ourselves vulnerable to help our neighbour? Are we willing to put our life in danger for the sake of our neighbour? The Samaritan, who was considered to be "far from God," nevertheless hears "the voice of God," and allows God to be the writer of his life—yes, the Samaritan changed his plans that night for God. This is at the *heart* of the Good Samaritan model.

———————————————

We can now see why most of us have moved away from the Good Samaritan model. Allowing *God to write our lives* can get very messy. I have plans. I have things to do. Do You really expect me to change all that at a whim? Do You?

So, what we have done to make ourselves feel better is to *politicize* the love we are called to give our neighbour. Let me explain by paraphrasing the words of the Catholic apologist and professor of philosophy, Peter Kreeft:

> Politicization . . . can make us sacrifice concrete persons to abstract and personal causes. We can even come to believe that we are Saints and heroes of charity, because our hearts bleed for people that we have never met in some faraway place, even while we unfortunately neglect the people that are closest to us. In other words, we not only run the risk, but we end up loving humanity instead of our neighbours.
>
> It is surprisingly easy for us to arrive at the state of mind where we are genuinely shocked if someone points out to us that not once does the Bible ever tell us to love humanity, that glimmering glorious abstract cloud of idealism.
>
> But instead, it always tells us to love our neighbour, that humdrum inconvenient unspectacular idiot that we live with. As a result, we end up practising what Charles Dickens calls telescopic philanthropy. That is, we end up looking at the world from the wrong end of the telescope, seeing the things that are near as far away, and the things that are far away as near. So

that the farther away a thing is, the more passionately concerned we are about it.[103]

| Peter Kreeft |

The model of the Good Samaritan challenges us. It is simple but very penetrating, and it keeps us from falling into this trap of loving *humanity* and ignoring our *neighbour*. In reality, the focus of the Good Samaritan model is *not* the love of humanity—in the abstract— it is solely focused on the love to our neighbour, *that humdrum inconvenient unspectacular idiot* standing in front of us. And yes, we should not be afraid to acknowledge that there are situations where that unspectacular idiot will get on our nerves. Nevertheless, we must see Christ in that unspectacular idiot. Moreover, we must know that Christ died for that unspectacular idiot.

In a way, it is easier to love "humanity" (someone halfway across the world) than to even deal with, let alone *agape* (ἀγάπη), the crazy neighbour standing in front of us (*Note*[104]). I think this is another reason that we have *politicized* the love we are called to give (*Note*[105]). For it is easier to get behind a cause in some faraway country with a sterile dispensation of monetary funds, in order to make ourselves feel good, rather than dealing with that smelly, unbathed person, or that annoying, trying person, or the attitude-filled, ungrateful person, or the rude, wretched, and nasty person, standing right in front of us. Again, it is precisely those *unspectacular idiots* whom we are called to *agape* (ἀγάπη), for they *are* our neighbours (*Note*[106]).

Even the Saints dealt with this. So, if we are in this situation, here is practical advice and an inspiring prayer from Saint Teresa of Calcutta:

> If you are in trouble, and quite compelled to do something for a person you dislike, do it like this . . . [Say] "I do it for You," starting with "I" on the little finger, ended with "You" on the thumb. The five fingers touched for the five words. Commit your work to God and say to yourself, "God, this work I am not doing for the wretched person. I do it for

CHARITY AND THE GOOD SAMARITAN MODEL

You." And do it for God. Let your mind be an instrument of His will and your hands do His work.[107] When you speak, look at the person in front of you. Say this prayer in your mind: Jesus, be now in this person when I speak to him and help me to see You in him. Bless me, so that I may speak to him with all sincerity, as I would speak to You. Look at me through his eyes and help me to succeed. If I fail to please You in this person, give me courage that I can bear the pain meekly and cheerfully.[108]

| Saint Teresa of Calcutta |

True *agape* (ἀγάπη) hurts. It is painful. It takes us out of our comfort zone. It lives according to the Beatitudes.[109] It is action over words. It is concrete, not abstract in its works. Thus, it follows the model of the Good Samaritan.

Remember, the Good Samaritan parable comes at the heels of the twofold commandment "You shall love the Lord, your God, with all your heart, with all your being, with all your strength, and with all your mind, and your neighbour as yourself" (Lk 10:27). As mentioned, this acknowledges that we cannot *agape* (ἀγάπη) God without loving our neighbour, and conversely, we cannot love our neighbour without the *agape* (ἀγάπη) of God (*Note*[110]). The twofold commandment is connected, yet separate. We should not merge them into one nor view them as two. It is in this context, and to answer the self-justifying question from the scholar of the law, "who is my neighbour?" (Lk 10:29), that Jesus gives us this parable (Lk 10:30–37). Subtly, Jesus also flips the question (Lk 10:36), from "Who *is* my neighbour?" to in essence "Who *was* a neighbour to the other?" This challenges and invites us *to be* a neighbour to all and to see *all* as neighbour to us (*Note*[111]).

I agree that although this model is simple, it is really difficult to follow. However, true Christian love must be actualized in a concrete demonstration of love (cf. Jms 2:17 and Mt 25:35–36). Yes, this is difficult, but this is what we are called to do: "Amen, I say to you, whatever you did for one of these least brothers of mine, you did for Me" (Mt 25:40; also cf. Isa 1:17, Deut 10:18, and Jms 1:27). The

Good Samaritan model is Jesus' "pastoral program" for us. So, let us go and be a neighbour to all.

———————

Now, as talked about, merely helping our neighbour is inadequate. It is a good thing to do, but it is still insufficient. The Good Samaritan model is consequently a lifestyle. It is a lifestyle centred not on ourselves, but on the other—that particular person we meet in our in our day-to-day life. Likewise, helping our neighbour must be in Christ and thus becomes a part of the way we live, a giving of our very self. Pope Benedict XVI makes this connection. In these words, listen and ponder carefully this inner movement, this disposition that is required of us:

> My deep personal sharing in the needs and sufferings of others becomes a sharing of my very self with them: if my gift is not to prove a source of humiliation, I must give to others not only something that is my own, but my very self; I must be personally present in my gift.[112]
>
> | Pope Benedict XVI |

He then takes it a step further:

> Indeed, to accept the "other" who suffers means that I take up his suffering in such a way that it becomes mine also . . . In the end, even the "yes" to love is a source of suffering, because love always requires expropriation of my "I," in which I allow myself to be pruned and wounded.[113]
>
> | Pope Benedict XVI |

Do you see the subtle yet profound movement that is asked of us? As alluded, the model of the Good Samaritan goes beyond just helping our neighbour. For it cannot stop there. We are called to a vocation to *agape* (ἀγάπη). We therefore allow this *expropriation* of ourselves, purely out of *agape* (ἀγάπη) for Christ and our neighbour.

CHARITY AND THE GOOD SAMARITAN MODEL

The Good Samaritan is a model of a joy-filled humble servant. We find our joy not in being served, but in serving others in humility, in Christ.

This is not something we can turn on or off. This help of our neighbour is a vocation, our "vocation to charity." Helping our neighbour is good, but it is not good enough from an *agape* (ἀγάπη) perspective, for it lacks roots. We as Christians are called to a deeper reality, one grounded and rooted in Christ Jesus. We are called to a *vocation* to *agape* (ἀγάπη)—a vocation to love our neighbour in Christ, in which we place our life at and for His service.

I once heard it said that it is common to hear of Christian men and women who desire leadership, authority, or honour within the Church. We, however, rarely hear of those who want to be humble servants. It is time we put away our ambitious thoughts and desires, associate with the lowly (Rom 12:16), and humbly serve our brothers and sisters in Christ.

You recall that the second image at the beginning of this study is that of Jesus washing His disciples' feet. You can see the interplay between this image and the image of the Good Samaritan. Both are rooted in being a servant to the other, in a joyful, humble giving without the sound of trumpets (cf. Mt 6:2). A profound thing to ponder is that Jesus washed Judas' feet. Although He knew Judas would betray Him (Jn 13:11), with all *humility*, as a *servant*, and (I would argue) with *joy* (for He was doing the will of His Father), He washes the feet of His betrayer. This is amazing! This is our calling.

So, let us "Go and do likewise" (Lk 10:37; also cf. Jn 13:14–15). We must continue His work, for we have been recreated *in* Christ to carry out His works, which He has entrusted to us (Eph 2:10 and 4:24). "Be slaves of Christ the Lord" (Col 3:24). Therefore, "whatever you do, do from the heart, with your whole being. Do it for the Lord and not for others" (Col 3:23). We must listen to His word, let Him live in us, and become doers of His word (*Note*[114]).

Staying within the context of the Good Samaritan model—the helping of our neighbour in their temporal needs (i.e., the corporal works of mercy) I address seven practical issues.

Issue Number 1: Serving vs. Enabling.[115] Many Christians have a hard time distinguishing between *serving/helping* our neighbour (also referred to as giving a hand *up*), with that of *enabling* our neighbour (also referred to as giving a hand *out*). A good definition that distinguishes the two is that *serving* is rooted in helping and empowering people to do what they are unable to do for themselves, whereas *enabling* is the act of doing things for people that they themselves are able to do—thus allowing our neighbour to continue living an unhealthy lifestyle, or avoid taking responsibility for their life. Therefore, if in *serving/helping* we are in actuality *enabling*, we may be encouraging weakness in our neighbour. This is not *agape* (ἀγάπη). That said, there is a fine line between the two.

Let us look at the saying, "Give a man a fish, and you will feed him for a day. Teach a man to fish, and you will feed him for a lifetime." Different variations of this saying exist, but the gist is that it is better to teach people to do a particular thing so they may learn and better their life than to do it for them.

The saying has merit. However, from a Christian point of view, we are actually called to do both. As we work at "teaching a man to fish," we must also "give a man a fish" until the skills of fishing are learned, so the "man" does not go hungry in the meantime (cf. Jms 2:15–16). With discernment, we must make sure we are *serving* and empowering our neighbour throughout this process of "giving him a fish," and not *enabling* our neighbour by doing the work that the "man" is capable of doing.

For the second point, let us refer to a familiar expression: "tough-love." *Serving/helping* our neighbour does not mean we have to be nice to them. It does not mean we have to tell them what they want to hear. Holding people accountable, loving our neighbour enough to tell them the right thing and help them do it, confronting our neighbour's sinful path and not *enabling* them to continue on that path is definitely in harmony with *agape* (ἀγάπη). In fact, as acknowledged, *agape* (ἀγάπη) may demand us to exercise these forms of tough-love.

Bear in mind; tough-love is empowerment. It is an encouragement. If we *truly* love our neighbour, we will not convey what is only in line with society, popular culture, groupthink, or what is politically correct—we will convey and communicate the truth (*Note*[116]).

Again, doing for people what they are capable of doing for themselves can lead them to other sins, such as laziness, idleness, complacency, or even entitlement, which may lead to a lack of self-worth (*Note*[117]). This is not *agape* (ἀγάπη). Creating an environment that abdicates personal responsibility is also not *agape* (ἀγάπη).

It is unpopular to say so, but in our society, we see *enabling* of our neighbour, not *serving* our neighbour, played out politically and socially. The political and social elite, in the name of "serving," create and have created, social programs that are actually *enabling*, thus immobilizing society. To society's detriment, this *enabling* is sadly at the root of some social programs, in which we have shunned individual responsibility. Consequently, this has created dependency, not empowerment. By *enabling* people, the societal-creed that motivated the individual "to be all that you can be" and encouraging the personal responsibility of the "pursuit of happiness" (*Note*[118]) is slowly replaced by an entitlement culture.

A political agenda that promises a succession of continuous entitlements has gradually made people worse off, rather than empowering them. As Christians, we must stay clear of this. Unfortunately, however, we have picked up this far-from-Christian mentality. We, as a Church, must reinvigorate this politically incorrect discussion to promote self-motivation and personal responsibility. As Saint Paul clearly puts it: "We instructed you that if anyone was unwilling to work, neither should that one eat" (2 Thes 3:10; also cf. 2 Thes 3:6–8). Harsh but true. Individual responsibility is a necessity. Therefore, we must distinguish between *serving* and *enabling* in our love for our neighbour, for *agape* (ἀγάπη) must empower, not suppress. As mentioned, it is a subtle distinction, so we must use prudence,[119] one of the four cardinal virtues.[120]

Issue Number 2: Indifference vs. Enabling. Here we have two extremes. These polarized opinions might seem similar to Issue Number 1, but a slight difference exists.

In the previous issue, it is usually unintentional (it is a mistake we make). In this issue, however, it is to some extent intentional (even within the Christian community). For example, pertaining to homelessness (a predominant problem in today's Western culture), two extremes of thought exist in society (and yes, even among Christians). The one extreme says that the homeless are just a group of lazy people who must get off their "anatomy" and get a job. The other extreme says to house them, clothe them, feed them, and give them everything they need, requiring no effort of their own. Both extremes are not in line with loving our neighbour (*Note*[121]).

If you agree with the former extreme—you think that the homeless are just a group of lazy people—I am not going to try to convince you otherwise; however, as a Christian, you are called to help them move away from this sin of sloth.[122] So, go and figure out a way to help them.

If you agree with the latter extreme, let me offer two additional thoughts to what was addressed above in Issue Number 1. First, as stated, *enabling* creates dependency. Therefore, if we are intentionally *enabling*, our help can be more about us than the person we are helping—we may actually be feeding our ego.

Second, as human beings, we tend to respect and take care of the things we own or earn. This is due to a sense of accomplishment. We thus need purpose or meaning, more than money. We need this purpose or meaning to justify our life (*Note*[123]). There is a natural relationship between purpose or meaning and responsibility (*Note*[124]). Therefore, we should help each other pursue responsibility.

Issue Number 3: Self-serving Trumpets. This admonition directly comes from Jesus:

> Take care not to perform righteous deeds in order that people may see them; otherwise, you will have no recompense from your heavenly Father. Therefore, when you give alms, do not blow a trumpet before you, as the hypocrites do in the, synagogues, [media], and in the streets to win the praise of others. Amen, I say to you, they have received their reward. But when you give alms, do not let your left hand know what your right is doing, so that your almsgiving may be secret. And your Father who sees in secret will repay you. (Mt 6:1–4)

Charity and the Good Samaritan Model

Unfortunately, in today's society, some of us are donating to various causes to receive (directly or indirectly) prestige and praise from our peers. On one level, we set up foundations with our names on them. On another level, we are caught up in fund-raisers, dinners, and banquets, with high overhead expenses, that treat ourselves more than those in need. In some extreme cases, we even *sound the trumpet* to feed our ego, to draw attention to ourselves, which subtly gives us the ability to pat ourselves on the back with praise and adoration on how generous and giving we are. This is not the example to follow. We need to stop desiring the praises of others, or this will be our reward (Mt 6:2).

By the way, we may argue that there is a paradox here. As stated, we are told not to blow our trumpets (Mt 6:2) and thus give in silence and in secret; but we are also called to be a light to the world (Mt 5:14–16), and thus let our light shine before others. So, how do we reconcile this? Well, we must recognize that it is all about our inner disposition. Namely, it is not about us. It is Christ's light that we are shining, not our own. As we might have heard, He is the Sun, and we the Bride, are the Moon. The moon has no light of its own; it only reflects the light of the sun. Therefore, not only should our giving (or even the works we do) always point to Him and reflect Him, it will also be visible on His terms, not ours, and thus, the visibility of our giving should not be our goal or an end in and of itself. Our giving should never be done in the hopes of its being or becoming visible. Our motivation, pleasure, and joy must be in *just* doing His work, for the *agape* (ἀγάπη) of Him—humbly and discreetly. Let us therefore question ourselves, and honestly ascertain if our giving is in silence. If not, change!

Issue Number 4: Giving from Our Poverty. To help us understand this particular issue—and acknowledging that there are different nuances to the story of the poor widow from the Gospel of Saint Mark—we shall explore this story from a certain perspective:

> Jesus sat down opposite the treasury and observed how the crowd put money into the treasury. Many rich people put in large sums. A poor widow also came and put in two small coins worth a few cents.

Calling His disciples to Himself, He said to them, "Amen, I say to you, this poor widow put in more than all the other contributors to the treasury. For they have all contributed from their surplus wealth, but she, from her poverty, has contributed all she had, her whole livelihood." (Mk 12:42–44; also cf. Lk 21:1–4)

The issue we face is that most of us give out of our surplus. The society in which we live has an abundance of resources—it is therefore difficult for most of us to give from our poverty. How then, can we emulate the poor widow's example?

To do this, we first need to detach ourselves emotionally and physically from material possessions and thus depend on God's providence.[125] Second, as pointed out in Issue Number 3, we must give and act in secret. Third, our giving should be sacrificial. Let us refer to the combination of these three things as *giving from our poverty*.

Practically speaking, we can accomplish this in a few different ways. First, we can do this by forgoing a material possession, which we desire, and then in secret, helping others with that money. We can also tangibly attach our giving to some material possessions that we want, and again in secret, give the difference away. In these examples, the first option is self-explanatory, the second not so much; therefore, let me explain the second option before we move on.

Say we want to buy a particular item (e.g., a house, car, electronic device, or furniture). Instead of buying what we can afford (or what we desire or want), we buy something of lesser value (but which can fulfill our need), then we give the difference away. By doing so, we are directly attached to that giving and detached from that material possession; it is therefore giving from our poverty, for it is not out of our surplus. It is also sacrificial, for we feel the pain of not having what we want, to give others what they need (*Note*[126]). Remember, we should concern ourselves with the sacrificial aspect of our giving, more than the quantity of our giving. Our giving must somehow cost us as it did the poor widow.

That being said, giving from our poverty does not necessarily have to be monetary. For example, when we present *Christ* to our neighbour, we give out of our poverty, for it shows God's providence

CHARITY AND THE GOOD SAMARITAN MODEL

in our life. As Saint Peter and Saint John tells the man who was crippled from birth: "I have neither silver nor gold, but what I do have I give you" (Acts 3:6)—and what they had was Christ (Acts 3:6–7). When we help our neighbours with their eternal needs, when we give them *Christ*, we are giving from our poverty.

Our *time* is another example of how we can give out of our poverty. When we share our time in the service of our neighbour (and allow God to control our time), in a manner speaking, we are giving out of our poverty, for we can never get back that time—it is irreplaceable. The time we give, however, must be in conjunction with our full attention—our presence. Giving our time is useless if we are distracted and not present to our neighbour (*Note*[127]). When we give our time and presence, we are actually giving all we have to His service. This also goes for the talents we have. We are not only called to use the talents and gifts God has given us for His glory, but also we will be held accountable for how we use these talents and how we multiply them for *His* sake (Mt 25:14–30).

One last point: some of us tend to wait to give until conditions are perfect. We bury our talents and say to ourselves, "Let me wait till the kids are all grown up, so I will have time," or, "Let me wait for my health to get better, so I will be of better service," or, "I just can't help others right now," for whatever reason. All these are just excuses—they go against giving from our poverty. Remember, this is not something that needs to be *formal*, but it needs to be a *way* of living, our daily life. Therefore, our giving should not feel like a duty or an obligation; it should be a *joy-filled reaction*. We manifest our most profound joy and fulfillment when we serve others in Christ, when we propagate His Kingdom, not ours.

Yes, this is challenging, and it takes discernment. However, do not let *discernment* immobilize us. I agree that this is not a black-and-white issue. In no way am I trying to give you a hard-and-fast answer on lifestyle questions. What I am suggesting is that with this insight, we must sit at the feet of Christ and reflect on what *He* wants of us.

We could easily make a valid argument that the poor widow should have kept one coin for herself. How could Jesus blame her if she did? But she did not! She recklessly gave everything she had. If we think about it, despite whatever situation we are in (as it happens, the more troublesome the situation we are in) if we find ourselves helping and giving despite our trials and tribulations, we will find ourselves following the poor widow's example (*Note*[128]). Jesus praises her example. Shouldn't we desire Jesus' praise?

Therefore in a way, there should be a sense of *recklessness* when we are giving from our poverty. This is the new standard. And yes, this is a paradox. On the one hand, we need to be prudent; but on the other hand, we should be reckless, carefree, and uncalculating in our giving, and thus emulate the poor widow's example.

Issue Number 5: Tithing. This issue is touchy and misunderstood (*Note*[129]). Unlike our Christian counterparts, Catholics do not tithe (in the formal sense of the word). That is, to tithe the first-fruits offering (Prov 3:9; also cf. Gen 4:4), or to tithe a percentage of income, usually 10 percent (Gen 14:20), as a consecration to God or for religious purposes (cf. Lev 27:30, Deut 14:22, Num 18:21, and 18:26).

We Catholics have created our uninformed reasons for this. We think the Catholic Church is abundant, so why should we give Her any more? We believe that tithing is an unnecessary Old Testament rule. We are selfish, consciously or subconsciously stating, "I earned this money, you didn't, so why should I have to share it with you?"

Now, interestingly, unlike some of our Christian counterparts, Catholics also hear little about tithing from our Church leaders. The reason for this, and the real reason that Catholics do not tithe (again in the formal sense of the word) is that even though we are called to provide for our Church's needs (*CCC* #2043; also cf. 2 Cor 9:5–8 and Canon Law 222 §1), which some of us may refer to as the tithing (in the informal sense of the word), we have no formal law requiring tithing in the New Testament (1 Cor 16:2), i.e., in the way of obligation. The point I am trying to make goes to *this* personal disposition that we must have. It is a realization that 100 percent of everything we have belongs to God.

Although the Old Testament called for first-fruits offering or 10 percent of earnings to be given to God (*Note*[130]), the deeper understanding within the Old Testament is that *all* belongs to Him (Deut 10:14 and 2 Chron 31:5). This understanding is clearly noted and realized in the New Testament (cf. Acts 4:32, Lk 18:22, and 2 Cor 8:2–4). Yes, 100 percent belongs to Him! Everything we have,

CHARITY AND THE Good Samaritan Model

everything we own, everything we earn is only through His grace, and therefore it is *all* technically His (1 Chron 29:14). For that reason, we must take everything we have and place it at His feet (Acts 4:34–35).

Once we do that, here is what happens. God, in His great generosity, gives a majority of it back to us (as stewards) and tells us that we may use it for our daily needs (Acts 4:34–35). A word of caution: even though we may use it freely, we must be careful about how we use it, for we are only stewards—it is still *all* His. We are thus accountable to Him (*Note*[131]).

Here is the summary in a practical sense. Our giving, for the Church's needs or to the poor, should not feel like an obligation—as a fulfillment of the law. Our giving should feel like an opportunity—as a fulfillment of love. We give because God has given us (graced us) with the ability and means to give (1 Pt 4:10). Everything we have is His; therefore, we should put it *all* to His service.

Issue Number 6: Charitable Organizations. Here we will look at donating via charitable organizations, or not-for-profits, or non-government organizations (NGO), and the like (*Note*[132]). Although, as stated, this is *not* what I am advocating in this chapter, for this should *not* be our primary mode of giving (and I hope that we are now discerning our calling, using the Good Samaritan model), I nonetheless recognize that for most of us, this has been our primary way of charitable giving. For that reason, this needs to be addressed.

The issue we face here is that some of these "charitable" organizations have become "big business"—which is unfortunate and somewhat ironic. Besides, they sometimes use the poor—or to state harshly, "sell the poor"—to support their big business. I do not want to take away from the good work that some of these organizations are doing, but *awareness* is necessary (*Note*[133]). In his encyclical *Caritas in Veritate* (Charity in Truth), Pope Benedict XVI addresses this issue:

> From this standpoint, international organizations might question the actual effectiveness of their bureaucratic and administrative machinery, which is often excessively costly. At times it happens that those who receive aid become subordinate to the aid-

givers, and the poor serve to perpetuate expensive bureaucracies which consume an excessively high percentage of funds intended for development.[134]

| Pope Benedict XVI |

Again, this calls us to use the virtue of prudence. Pope Benedict XVI tells us that we should ask organizations to

commit themselves to complete transparency, informing donors and the public of the percentage of their income allocated to programmes of cooperation, the actual content of those programmes and, finally, the detailed expenditure of the institution itself.[135]

| Pope Benedict XVI |

Issue Number 7: Do-good Philosophy (cf. Gal 3:1–14). The final issue I would like to discuss is this merit-based belief which some Christians have (i.e., of *doing good* so we can get into heaven, or earn any other reward, or a version of getting "brownie points" for our good acts).

Now, some of you might laugh at this, but I have heard it repeatedly. In fact, during my group presentations, I asked the question: "What can we do to get into heaven?" To this question, different "works" is often the answer I receive. I, however, rarely receive the answer: "nothing!"

Yes, there is nothing we can *do* to get into heaven—*absolutely nothing*. Think about it. If the good works we perform (whatever they may be) can achieve our salvation (get us into heaven), didn't Christ die for nothing? Be that as it may, I realize that some of you might not like this answer. For if I go to Mass every Sunday, pray the rosary daily, volunteer at my local food bank, give to various charities, and overall be a *good* person, I should get into heaven, shouldn't I? However, as it is written:

There is no one just, not one, there is no one who understands, there is no one who seeks God, all have gone astray; alike are worthless; there is not one who does good, there is not even one. (Rom 3:11–12; also cf. Ti 3:4–7)

All of us have sinned and come short of the glory of God. It is therefore only through the redemptive work of Christ Jesus and His grace that we are justified. For now, "the righteousness of God has been manifested . . . through faith in Jesus Christ" (Rom 3:21–22).

Pope Benedict XVI puts it well when he says, "the Kingdom of God is a gift. And we cannot—to use a classical expression—'merit' heaven through our works. Heaven is always more than we could merit."[136] We *cannot* save ourselves by our own efforts.

Now, some of you, with Bible in hand, are ready to ask: Aren't we going to be judged according to our deeds (Rev 20:12), by the *works* we did on this earth (Rom 2:6 and 1 Pt 1:17)? As we stand before the Judgment Seat of Christ, won't we receive recompense, according to what we did in the body (2 Cor 5:10)?

Well, what we have here is a paradox (*Note*[137]). On the one hand, our redemption is a gift, which comes solely through the merciful saving act of Jesus our Savior (cf. Ti 3:5-7), and is "not because of any righteous deeds we have done" (Ti 3:5). No, we cannot buy our salvation with good works! On the other hand, however, we must "work out [our] salvation with fear and trembling" (Phil 2:12).

I know that this might sound perplexing at first; therefore to illustrate this, we shall look at the words Jesus Himself uses in the Book of Revelation. Jesus commends the church in Ephesus for their works, by stating, "I know your works, your labour . . . you have endurance and have suffered for my name, and you have not grown weary" (Rev 2:2–3). Here the Greek word used for *works* is ἔργον (ergon/er'-gon), and the word used for *labour* is κόπος (kopos/kop'-os). Even though both of these words have multiple meanings, we can see conformity between *ergon* (ἔργον) and the corporal works of mercy; and that of *kopos* (κόπος) and the spiritual works of mercy.

The paradox here is that we must realize it is only by God's mercy, grace, and through faith in Christ Jesus that we are saved. However, we also must recognize that the faith we profess is not a mere internal reckoning, but must concretely manifest itself in works, *ergon* (ἔργον) and labours, *kopos* (κόπος), which in turn give credence to *this* faith. It is the loving reaction—or product—of our salvation that we have received. This is a compulsory harmonic movement from one to the other. If not, as Saint James argues, our faith is nothing; it is useless, it is dead (Jms 2:14ff.).

Here is another way of looking at it using Saint Paul's first letter to the Corinthian community. In which, he clearly tells us that Christ Jesus *is* the foundation (cf. Rom 15:20), and no one can lay a foundation other than He (1 Cor 3:10-11). He is our salvation—period. However, we as Christians build upon that foundation "with gold, silver, precious stones, wood, hay, or straw" (1 Cor 3:12).

Yes, each one of us builds upon that foundation using the talents given to us. We must therefore pursue these works (our individual task and mission), with ardent care, for each one of our works "will come to light" (1 Cor 3:13). Yes, we will not only be accountable for our work (what we have done, and what we have not done), we will also be tested for the quality of our works (1 Cor 3:13).

But keep in mind that conversely, "All our good deeds are like polluted rags," filthy soiled garments (Is 64:5). This speaks to our very nature; that, even in our good works, actions, or righteous acts, we have hidden intentions. That said—filthy and soiled as they are— if our faith does not result in works, or if we do not pursue these works in Christ Jesus, we are no better than the demons (cf. Jms 2:19).

So reiterating, the works *ergon* (ἔργον), and labours *kopos* (κόπος) that we perform *are* a necessary manifestation of our faith— we will be accountable, and we will be tested for the quality of these works. However, these works do not *save* us (the works we do can never merit salvation in and of themselves); it is a concrete demonstration of the faith we have, and it is an absolutely necessary and integral part of our faith.

Unfortunately, this paradox has been muddied by Martin Luther's "faith alone" (*Note*[138]) argument for the past five centuries (*Note*[139]). The back-and-forth of this argument has created many misunderstandings and misconceptions of the actual Christian teaching on the subject (*Note*[140]).

Let me summarize the real understanding of this paradox and segue into the next chapter, using the words of Saint Paul:

[It is] by free grace (God's unmerited favour) that you are saved (delivered from judgment and made partakers of Christ's salvation) through [your] faith. And this [salvation] is not of yourselves [of your own doing, it came not through your own striving], but it is the gift of God.

Not because of works [not the fulfillment of the law's demands], lest any man should boast. [It is not the result of what anyone can possibly do, so no one can pride himself in it or take glory to himself.] For we are God's [own] handiwork, His workmanship, recreated in Christ Jesus, [born anew] that we may do those good works which God predestined (planned beforehand) for us [taking paths which He prepared ahead of time], that we should walk in them [living the good life which He prearranged and made ready for us to live]. (Eph 2:8–10)[14]

In our temporal life *agape* (ἀγάπη) is revealed as mercy.
Therefore, the mercy He shows us, we must in turn, show others.

Chapter 7 | Charity and Mercy

As I was working on this book (on March 13, 2015), the Church announced a Holy Year of Mercy, which was to commence on December 8, 2015 (the Solemnity of the Immaculate Conception) and ending on November 20, 2016 (the Solemnity of Christ the King). Inspired and challenged by this, I thought it would be beneficial to look at *mercy* within its own chapter.

During this Year of Mercy, Pope Francis also published a question-and-answer-style book titled *The Name of God Is Mercy*. In this book, he quotes the following teaching from his predecessor, Pope Benedict XVI, which was given during a Regina Caeli address on Divine Mercy Sunday (March 30, 2008). It is as follows:

> Indeed, mercy is the central nucleus of the Gospel message; it is the very name of God, the Face with which He revealed Himself in the Old Covenant and fully in Jesus Christ, the incarnation of Creative and Redemptive Love. May this merciful love also shine on the face of the Church and show itself through the sacraments, in particular that of Reconciliation, and in works of charity, both communitarian and individual. May all that the Church says and does manifest the mercy God feels for man, and therefore for us. When the Church has to recall an unrecognized truth or a betrayed good, She always does so impelled by merciful love, so that men and women may have life and have it abundantly (cf. Jn 10:10). From Divine Mercy, which brings peace to hearts, genuine peace flows into the world, peace between different peoples, cultures, and religions.[142]
>
> | Pope Benedict XVI |

In these words, we can see a relationship between mercy and charity (Christian love). I want to examine this relationship within this context, for as it has been said, "Charity has one action, and that action is mercy" (*Note*[143]).

———————◆———————

Before we begin, however, even with this inspiration, I struggle when I write this. Mercy is complex. It can be confusing and easily misunderstood. No matter how we define it, however, I know that I have been far from merciful—this is a continual struggle. Some of you may relate to my confusion and conflict. Nevertheless, we know our calling and God's requirements. So, with the grace of God and in His timing, let us pray for each other as we move forward in this chapter.

Let me clarify three things before we continue. First, in our next chapter, we state, God *is* love. There is a relationship between mercy and love. Therefore, does that mean we can say, God *is* mercy? Well, not really. We can only say that God is mercy insofar as its connection with love. To state, "God *is* mercy" unequivocally (in the same manner that we proclaim, "God *is* love") is problematic.

To be precise, we can say, God is mercy only after sin entered humanity (*Note*[144]). God was *not* mercy prior to the entrance of sin, for mercy is an aspect of love or an attribute of God that was only required after sin entered (*Note*[145]).

Second, and connected to the first, *agape* (ἀγάπη) is revealed in the temporal life as *mercy*. As written in the encyclical *Dives in Misericordia* (*On the Mercy of God*):

> In the eschatological fulfillment mercy will be revealed as love, while in the temporal phase, in human history, which is at the same time the history of sin and death, love must be revealed above all as mercy and must also be actualized as mercy. Christ's messianic program, the program of mercy, becomes the program of His people, the program of the Church.[146]
>
> | Saint Pope John Paul II |

Third, the word *mercy* can be misconstrued. Therefore, it would be beneficial to first look at what mercy is *not*. Mercy is not *acceptance* as this word has been used in our politically correct society. Neither is mercy a form of *relativism*, in the way of "You, have your 'truth,' and I have mine. I will not impose my 'truth' on you; by this, I am showing mercy towards you." Mercy is also not *approval* of sinful human behaviour; that is a misinterpretation of the "Who am I to judge" statement that we discussed earlier (in Chapter 3, Charity: It is Ethical and Moral). Mercy is not *injustice*; it does not cancel out justice, in the sense that justice (legally or judicially speaking) is somehow done away with or usurped. Mercy does not call something that *is* just unjust, nor something that *was* just is now somehow unjust; that is, "we should not fall into a false understanding that what was once 'good' is now 'bad,' the Church doesn't evolve out of a true teaching, nor does humanity progress beyond natural law."[147] Mercy is not *submission*, as in the condoning of a secular narrative or a particular ideology. In addition, mercy is not *subjective*—that is, mercy cannot be void of Truth.

It is unfortunate that when the Church speaks of *mercy*, some see it as condoning sinful actions, or even abrogating justice itself. No, we need not lower the moral bar when we speak of mercy. The Church must always present an objectively high moral standard or ideal. She must clearly articulate this demanding standard. However, simultaneously She must express Her mercy in an equally clear and demanding standard. It is *not* one or the other it is always both. The Year of Mercy, therefore, is not a Year of Acceptance, nor a Year of Anything Goes. It is as stated: A Year of Mercy—which includes an extremely high objective moral standard in concert with the demands of mercy (*Note*[148]).

I realize that some of these statements need to be unpacked. So, we will do this systematically, starting with defining *mercy*.

In Hebrew, there are two predominant words used for mercy. The first Hebrew word is חֶסֶד (chêsêd/*kheh'-sed*). This word is transliterated into English as *hesed*. The second Hebrew word is רָחַם (râcham/*raw-kham'*); it is transliterated into English as *rahamim* (*Note*[149]). As we have seen with the word *love*, here we translate these two different words and their meanings into only one English word: *mercy*.

According to *Mounce's Dictionary*, *hesed* (חֶסֶד) "is one of the richest, most theologically insightful terms in the Old Testament."[150] Therefore, *hesed* (חֶסֶד) "cannot be adequately translated in many languages, including English" Gordon Clark would concur, also adding that *hesed* (חֶסֶד) "is not merely an attitude or an emotion; it is an emotion that leads to an activity beneficial to the recipient."[151] For it not only denotes kindness, loving-kindness, love, loyal-love, loyalty, and mercy, but also it most poignantly denotes covenant-love, "employed in the context of relationship between God and humans as well as between one human and another"[152]—in which the recipient is the beneficiary. In addition, in this Hebrew word, we have not only the meaning for *grace* (*Note*[153]) and mercy (*Note*[154]) as a gift but the legal quality or the *justice* of mercy.

However, when translating *hesed* (חֶסֶד) into Greek (the Septuagint), the translators used the Greek word ἔλεος (eleos/*el'-eh-os*). In turn, Saint Jerome translates it into the Latin word *misericordia*. Both the *eleos* (ἔλεος) and *misericordia* predominantly mean "mercy" as in English. We should note that *eleos* (ἔλεος) is linked to the Greek word *agape* (ἀγάπη) and *misericordia* is linked to its Latin equivalent, *cāritās* (charity) (*Note*[155]). With this, we can see how the English word *mercy* (which is rooted in the Latin word *misericordia*) is also linked to love.

The second Hebrew word is *rahamim* (רָחַם). According to *Mounce's Dictionary*, this word means "to have compassion on, show mercy, take pity on; to find compassion, be loved; feelings of compassion are usually accompanied by acts of compassion."[156] This act of compassion is a love from the *womb*, so to speak, because *rahamim* (רָחַם) is rooted in motherly love. It is therefore a mercy that is unmerited and undeserved.

As mentioned, we see a combination of both *hesed* (חֶסֶד) and *rahamim* (רָחַם) in our English word, mercy. Now that we understand these two definitions, we can move forward and look at mercy in two core categories.

The first we can call *divine mercy*, which is the mercy God shows us. A vivid example of this is found in Saint John's Gospel in the story of the adulterous woman (Jn 8:3ff.). The second is *human*

WITNESS OF CHARITY

mercy, which is the mercy we show one another. For an example of this, we can look to the parable of the unforgiving servant, found in the Gospel of Saint Matthew (Mt 18:23ff.).

From a Christian perspective, we need to understand the former (divine mercy) to grasp the latter (human mercy)—or even to make sense of human mercy. For that reason, we shall begin with divine mercy.

"In the Old Testament, mercy is predicated of God (Deut 7:9), and His attitude toward the repentant sinner is mercy rather than punishment."[157] Divine mercy is real (Ex 34:6, Ps 86:15, and 103:8), and Jesus *is* the face of this reality. Despite our human parents' disobedience (Gen 3:6), a promise of mercy is given (Gen 3:15), and in the fullness of time, this promise is carried out *in* and *through* Christ Jesus (Gal 4:4). This is the reality of divine mercy; it is *the* act of a God who saves us. We would *not* exist, the cosmos would not exist without God's *agape* (ἀγάπη), without God's mercy, without God's grace, without God's forgiveness, without God's saving act (Gen 6:5–7, Isa 48:9, and Ex 32:9–14). Yes, God holds us in existence despite our sinful nature. Jesus gives Himself to us and for us. Jesus forgives us, despite us. Yes, despite us (Eph 2:1–10). In divine mercy, we see the *gift* of mercy from the word *hesed* (חֶסֶד), and we see the mercy that is *unmerited* and *undeserved* from the word *rahamim* (רַחַם). This is divine mercy!

It is worth underscoring that in the accurate and objective sense of the word, *only* Jesus can *forgive* (Acts 10:43), and it is only Jesus who forgives (Mt 9:2–7). It is only divine mercy that can confer true and objective forgiveness.

Therefore this forgiveness (because it is divine forgiveness) is a gift; it is gratuitous, it is unmerited, it is not of our own doing, it far surpasses any sin, and it is the only forgiveness that can bring us salvation (*Note*[158]).

Keeping this in mind, let us continue by looking at human mercy, which is usually understood in two different ways. The first is kindness or the help we give to people who are in desperate or bad situations. From a Christian point of view, we could call this the corporal works of mercy; for here, "mercy sees the distress of others, identifies with it, and seeks to overcome it as one seeks to have one's own suffering, guilt, and burdens overcome with the aid and assistance of others."[159] The second is the forgiving treatment of someone who could or should be treated harshly. From a Christian point of view, we could call this the spiritual works of mercy, for here, we see the gratuitous nature of mercy.

If you notice, I am qualifying this from a "Christian point of view" because Christian mercy must move beyond *mere* human mercy. Christian mercy *is* divinely inspired and is a manifestation of divine mercy. Therefore, Christian mercy inherently goes beyond the general understanding of human mercy.

To elaborate, the corporal works of mercy, lifted up in Christ, reveal Christian love. The spiritual works of mercy, lifted up in Christ, embody divine mercy. To be clear, if the mercy we give is *not* connected to divine mercy it will only lead us to vanity and pride.

Let us summarize before we continue. We first noted that there are two Hebrew words for mercy: *hesed* (חֶסֶד) and *rahamim* (רַחֲמִים). Second, we categorized two types of mercy: divine mercy and human mercy. Then we acknowledged that human mercy could be demonstrated in two different ways, which we call (from a Christian point of view), the corporal and spiritual works of mercy. With this, we further concluded that Christian mercy differs from mere human mercy, for it is connected to the Divine. Consequently, we can now conclude that Christian mercy is therefore *objective*, for it is rooted in the Divine, in Truth.

Why are these categories relevant? How do they apply to us? To answer this, we will return to the concept of divine mercy and work our way through it.

———————

God loves us, and He shows that *agape* (ἀγάπη) in and through Jesus via mercy. Jesus does not want to condemn us; Jesus wants to save us—all of us (1 Tm 2:3–4). In and through the mercy of God, salvation is not only open to *all* (*Note*[160]), God desires that it be accepted by *all* (Rom 10:13 and Acts 2:21).

Mercy is not this crazy notion that our sinful behaviour is acceptable (*Note*[161]). In reality, it is the exact opposite. We recognize that an objective moral order exists. We realize that we are responsible for our actions. Therefore, we place ourselves at the feet of Christ, realizing our own wretchedness, our own sinfulness, and our own brokenness—we ask for His mercy and forgiveness (Note[162]). No! We beg for His mercy and forgiveness. We beat our breasts without even looking up to Him, we beg (Lk 18:13). Within this act of realization and begging, we are given His mercy; we are not condemned.

On the one hand, the Church must state sin as sin, and thus condemn sin; for She must always convey the truth. On the other hand, and in unison, She must hold the sinner in Her arms and convey God's infinite mercy. No human sin is beyond the forgiveness of God. God will receive any and all who seek Him.

With His mercy, we now move forward. That is to say, we must now *show* others mercy (i.e., the corporal works of mercy), and more importantly, we must *lead* others to the fullness of divine mercy (i.e., through the spiritual works of mercy). The mercy we have received (divine mercy) is the mercy we give through the corporal and spiritual works of mercy (Note[163]).

It is vital that we comprehend this truth, in this order: first, that we are sinners, we need to be saved, and we *need* His mercy; second, that we cannot receive His mercy without *asking* (God's mercy is endless, all we need to do is desire and want His mercy); and third, that we must *give* what we have received, we cannot hoard it—"How shalt thou hope for mercy, rendering none?" Shakespeare asks in his play *The Merchant of Venice*.

Another quick summary: as Christians, we take part in divine mercy. The mercy we give to our neighbours, and our enemies, is therefore objective, for it is rooted in Truth. It is not subjective, based on our whims or personal judgment as to who deserves it. We show mercy towards the other, because of the mercy He has first shown us (Mt 18:23ff.), which is an act motivated by what we have received. If we do not give this mercy to others, the mercy that we have received from Him will be rescinded (Mt 18:32–35 and Jms 2:13).

God's action towards us is no mere abstraction—it is concrete. Therefore, our action must follow His, in which His love (and mercy) is made visible and tangible. We firmly stand on God's mercy. Thus, we give freely to all those who ask. Why? Because He has shown us, and is *continually* showing us, His unconditional mercy. We must go forth and become that sign of mercy towards others.

CHARITY AND MERCY

Please, do not misunderstand the word *unconditional*. Unconditional does not mean, "no matter what we do." Mercy is not automatically given to us (*Note*[164]). "The sinner should not presume that God will automatically or mechanically offer divine mercy."[165] Three *concrete* conditions are placed on us: first, we must recognize our need for mercy; second, we must ask for it; and third, we must in turn show mercy to others, or the mercy that we have received will be taken away.

In addition, *unconditional* does not mean that God does not have a choice (Ps 135:6; also cf. Jn 5:21). For God can show mercy to whomever He wishes (Ex 33:19; also cf. Rom 9:15). Stating, "God can do as He wishes" does not make Him capricious, arbitrary, or unjust (Rom 9:6–24). I am not arguing this; I am merely stating a biblical truth (*Note*[166]). "Whatever the LORD wishes He does in heaven and on earth" (Ps 135:6). We cannot and should not limit God or put Him in a box. It is also futile to assume that we *totally* understand His thinking (cf. Job 15:8 and Wisdom 9:13).

May I also suggest that we look at the issue from another perspective by turning this around and placing the onus on ourselves? However before we do this, it would be beneficial for us to understand the meaning of *justice*.

What is justice? In Hebrew, three words are used for justice. The first two are צֶדֶק (tsedeq/*tseh'-dek*) and צְדָקָה (ts⁼dâqâh/*tsed-aw-kaw'*); both are rooted in the Hebrew word צָדַק (tsâdaq/*tsaw-dak'*). These words denote righteousness, rightness, justness, just, virtuous, virtue, with the underlying root word (being a verb) adding the action *to be*, i.e., to be righteous, to be just, to be virtuous, and so forth. According to *Mounce's Dictionary,* these words are generally defined as

> the state or quality of that which accords with some recognized standard . . . Righteousness is first and foremost a quality ascribed to God. His actions are right and just. He hates wickedness and loves

WITNESS OF CHARITY

righteousness . . . God wants His people to pattern their lives after Him. Therefore, He wants them to live righteous lives; both religiously and morally.[167]

| *Mounce's Dictionary* |

With this understanding, from this point forward in our discussion of justice, I will refer to *this* form of justice, in its application of God's justice, as His *righteousness*, i.e., God's justice (righteousness).

It is important to note that this form of justice also applies to us, especially from a moral theology point of view (*Note*[168]). Justice, in this sense, is about right conduct and thus living our lives justly and righteously. It is also about right order in our lives and our relationships, in particular, our covenant-relationship with God.

The third Hebrew word for justice is מִשְׁפָּט (mishpât/*mish-pawt'*); this denotes the legal or judicial quality of justice, i.e., judicial pronouncement, judgment, ruling, verdict, legal proceedings before the court, conflict resolution, penalty, the charge of a crime, and laws or commandments (*Note*[169]).

From this point forward, I will refer to *this* form of justice, in its application of God's justice, as His *judicial justice*, i.e., God's justice (judicial).

Again, we should note that this form of justice also applies to us; however, we must be cautious in dispensing this form of justice to others. Either we must refrain from exercising this justice (*Note*[170]), or with certitude, we must be confident that we are correctly dispensing God's justice (judicial), in *agape* (ἀγάπη):

> I charged your judges at that time, "Listen to complaints among your kinsmen, and administer true justice [*tsedeq* (צֶדֶק)—righteousness] to both parties even if one of them is an alien. In rendering justice [*mishpât* (מִשְׁפָּט)—judicial], do not consider who a person is; give ear to the lowly and to the great alike, fearing no man, justice [*mishpât* (מִשְׁפָּט)—judicial] is God's." (Deut 1:16–17)

It is this justice, *mishpât* (מִשְׁפָּט), in the form of judgment or judging others, which I spoke of in Chapter 3, Charity: It is Ethical and Moral, and I will also talk of it later in this chapter.

Now, again, returning to God's justice, these two distinctions are important: namely, when we speak of God's justice, are we speaking of God's justice (righteousness) or God's justice (judicial)? With either the former or latter, we can proclaim without hesitation that God is just, because truth, reason, and fairness are inherent in His nature. We can further state that God's justice (righteousness) is demonstrated through His mercy. However, when speaking of God's justice (judicial), we would have to place His justice in opposition to His mercy. For God may act in justice (judicial) or in justice (righteousness). His justice (judicial) is nevertheless still rooted in His *agape* (ἀγάπη), for He cannot act in injustice, for this violates His justice (righteousness). Now, God may not want to demonstrate His justice (judicial) through His justice (righteousness) and His mercy. However, we should not confuse this as injustice; or by His demonstrating His justice (judicial), we should not confuse this as unloving or unmerciful, for He cannot go against Himself—He cannot go against His justice (righteousness). Keep in mind that *both* His justice (righteousness) and His justice (judicial) are *rooted* in His love (*Note*[171]).

On a side note, this understanding can help us work through a multitude of errors. One such error that comes to mind (which I will elaborate in the next chapter, Charity: The Ultimate Source), is this notion held by Christians that there is an Old Testament God and a New Testament God. When we understand, however, God's justice (judicial) and His justice (righteousness), it can help us realize that there is no such thing as an Old and New Testament God.

Here is the understanding; God gave us the law to show us what sin *is* (Rom 5:13) and, thus, how sinful we are (Rom 3:20). However, God desired to reveal His justice (righteousness) independently and apart from the law (Rom 3:21), in His Son. So, if we acknowledge our sinfulness and ask God for His justice (righteousness) in Christ Jesus, He will pour out that justice (righteousness) upon us, which is His mercy (1 Jn 1:8–9). That is to say, when we recognize our need for His mercy (in faith), and ask for His mercy, we will be justified in Him (Rom 5:1–11); e.g., think of the criminal (the good thief) that was crucified with Jesus (Lk 23:42). However, if we claim self-righteousness, we will be choosing God's justice (judicial). Therefore, we will be judged according to the law (Rom 2:12). But do not fool yourself; "do not nullify the grace [or mercy] of God, for if justification comes through the law, then Christ died for nothing" (Gal 2:21). God's grace or mercy reigns through justification through Christ Jesus (Rom 5:21). "Mercy does not override justice [judicial], but rather transcends it and converts the sinner into a just person by bringing about repentance and openness to the Holy Spirit."[172]

With this understanding and distinctions, let us return to the statement "God can do as He *wishes.*" Here is the amazing thing: God allows us to *participate* in what He *wishes.* Because of His love for us, that is what He precisely *wishes* to do—to give us (all of us) free will and thus to allow *us* to make that decision. As stated, therefore the *onus* is on us.

In His justice, in His righteousness, in His justness, He gives us a gift (an unmerited, undeserved, gratuitous gift), which is His mercy. But He does not stop there! He does not *force* this gift upon us. Just as He does not *force* His love on us, He likewise does not *force* His mercy on us. Yes, He allows us to choose! This is the astonishing part of His *agape* (ἀγάπη): He lets us decide. Do we want this gift, His justice (righteousness)? Or do we want to choose His justice (judicial)? Yes, we can be judged according to His justice (righteousness), which is demonstrated to us as His mercy; or according to His justice (judicial), which will be given in love according to the law (Rom 2:12). Due to the lavishness of His *agape* (ἀγάπη), the choice is ours to make (*Note*[173]). Chapter 5, Charity and the Law, is precisely this. If we decide to be judged by His justice (judicial), the law will judge us. If, however, we choose to be judged by His justice (righteousness)—His mercy—we will be judged (or are being judged) by the new understanding and interpretation of the law, that is to say, the *law of love* (cf. CCC #1972).

So, to repeat, if we decide to be judged by His righteousness, we first need to acknowledge that we need His righteousness, we need His mercy; then we ask for His mercy; and once we ask for it, we *will* receive it (Mt 21:22 and Mk 11:24). Then we must give what we have received, for we must "speak and so act as people who will be judged by the law of freedom" (Jms 2:12). Or we can choose to be judged by His justice (judicial), by the law itself (and thus we must keep the law—every letter of the law). The decision is ours to make: do we want to be judged by freedom's law, the law of love, the law of grace, the law of mercy, the law of His righteousness; or do we want to be judged by the law itself, the law of His justice (judicial)?

Remember, mercy is something that we should not have received under normal circumstances. We receive something that we do not deserve. In recognition of our sinfulness, we stand off at a distance, not even looking to the heavens, beat our breasts, and pray, "O God, be merciful to me a sinner" (Lk 18:13). We realize that we deserve nothing good from God; therefore, we ask for His mercy. To receive His mercy, we need to ask for it (Mt 7:8 and Lk 11:9–10). If we do not ask for His mercy, we will receive His justice (judicial). God loves us, but He will not force His *agape* (ἀγάπη) on us. Listen, and ponder these words:

> "God created us without us: but He did not will to save us without us" [Saint Augustine]. To receive His mercy, we must admit our faults. "If we say we have no sin, we deceive ourselves, and the truth is not in us. If we confess our sins, He is faithful and just, and will forgive our sins and cleanse us from all un-righteousness" [1 Jn 1:8–9]. (*CCC* #1847)

Yes, this is how much our God loves us! Mercy does not abrogate justice, but in a manner of speaking mercy is the fullness of God's truth; nevertheless, as noted, He will not force it upon us (*Note*[174]).

With that understanding, two extremes must be avoided. The one extreme is cheapening His mercy (this is an underlying attitude usually unarticulated, and sometimes even subconscious), in which we assume or presume that mercy is a *given*. This extreme attitude says, "It does not matter what I do, God in His infinite mercy will forgive me; I need no repentance, no responsibility, no μετανοέω (metanoeō/*met-an-o-eh'-o*) or call to conversion, for God is all loving and merciful" (*Note*[175]). No, "the message of God's mercy is not a message of cheap grace" Cardinal Walter Kasper exclaims.[176] The other extreme is to imply directly or indirectly that we need to work for our mercy, or it is somehow up to us to achieve it. This extreme attitude says, "I deserve His mercy because I work for it."

Even the hint of either extreme must be avoided (*Note*[177]). Do not cheapen mercy; mercy cost God the death of His Son. And, do not think for a moment that our own merits can attain mercy; it is a free gift from our loving God.

For further clarification and application, we will now turn to three of the main parables dealing with mercy (and forgiveness): the parable of the unforgiving servant (Mt 18:21–35), the parable of the prodigal son (Lk 15:11–32), and the parable of the workers in the vineyard (Mt 20:1–16). And, we will also look at three aspects of mercy. These three parables and three aspects highlight the different nuances of mercy, which we have discussed. Let us begin with the three parables:

Parable Number 1: The Unforgiving Servant (Mt 18:21–35). Jesus shares this parable on the heels of a question from Saint Peter: "Lord, if my brother sins against me, how often must I forgive him? As many as seven times?" (Mt 18:21). To this question, Jesus gives an astonishing answer: "I say to you, not seven times but seventy-seven times" (Mt 18:22) (*Note*[178]). He is saying to Saint Peter (and by extension to you and me) as long as our brother or sister asks for forgiveness, we must forgive him or her without limit. Why? Why should we forgive without limit? Because our Lord has forgiven us (Eph 4:32), so, we are called to do the same (Col 3:13 and Mt 6:14–15).

It has been said that forgiveness, rooted in mercy is an entry point to *agape* (ἀγάπη). Forgiveness opens our hearts so we may *agape* (ἀγάπη) those who have hurt us and not seek their demise. Forgiveness is when we grant a pardon to the person who has offended us, when we stop the feelings of resentment towards that person, when we cancel off their debt (cf. Mt 6:12), and when we wipe the slate clean. Forgiveness is "not eager for revenge"—*Non cupidi vindicate*—state the Early Church Fathers. Forgiveness, in the words of Saint Francis de Sales, is "surrendering our natural desire for revenge and redemption."[179] By doing this, we move into *agape* (ἀγάπη) where we will the good of the other, thus forgo hatred and hostility, through forgiveness and mercy.

With this, Jesus recounted the parable: "That is why the kingdom of heaven may be likened to a king who decided to settle accounts with his servants. When he began the accounting, a debtor was brought before him who owed him a huge amount" (Mt 18:23–24). The amount specified here is ten thousand talents. Some scholars state that this was equivalent to 160 years of wages in Jesus' time, and others convert this amount to approximately 3.6 billion dollars in our time. At any rate, as stated, this was a massive sum of money. So,

> since he had no way of paying it back, his king ordered him to be sold, along with his wife, his children, and all his property, in payment of the debt. At that, the servant fell down, did him homage, and said, "Be patient with me, and I will pay you back in full." (Mt 18:25–26)

Again, this sum of money, this debt, was so vast that it was impossible to repay, which is akin to the debt we owe our King; an amount so huge we cannot pay it, even in due time. Therefore, just like our King, this king, "moved with compassion . . . let him go, and forgave him the debt" (Mt 18:27). Despite this, "when that servant had left, he found one of his fellow servants who owed him a much smaller amount" (Mt 18:28), only one hundred denarii—to put this amount into perspective, it was about one hundred days' wages, or about six thousand dollars in our time, not an insignificant amount of money, but nothing compared to what he owed, and what was just forgiven him. Nevertheless, "he seized him and started to choke him, demanding, 'Pay back what you owe.' Falling to his knees, his fellow servant begged him, 'Be patient with me, and I will pay you back'" (Mt 18:28–29). Now it may have been possible for his fellow servant to pay, for it was relatively a small amount.

But he refused. Instead, he had him put in prison until he paid back the debt. When his fellow servants saw what had happened, they were deeply disturbed; [they] went to their king and reported the whole affair. His king summoned him and said to him, "You wicked servant! I forgave you your entire debt because you begged me. Should you not have had pity on your fellow servant, as I had pity on you?" Then, in anger, his king handed him over to the torturers until he should pay back the whole debt. (Mt 18:30–34)

You may ask, "How does torture lead to repayment?" Well, some suggest that the torture is self-imposed. That is to say, when we adamantly refuse or do not show mercy (forgive others) from *our heart*, this affects us mentally and physically. Thus we *torture* ourselves. We can see this reality within our own lives or those around us. Also, when we refuse or resist forgiving others, we are refusing or resisting God's love; thus, we are torturing ourselves— again this is self-imposed.

The theological interpretation, however, is as follows: as mentioned, the first servant's debt, like our debt (*Note*[180]) to our Lord, was so vast that it could not be repaid (cf. Ps 49:8–9). Therefore, giving him time for repayment was pointless, for his debt was *unpayable*. As a result, there are only two options, forgive the debt completely (which is a gift of mercy—a demonstration of love) or *endless* punishment. The first option was exercised, then rescinded, and the second option was given. Our lesson: we should not take God's mercy for granted. Why?

Here is the central teaching, for Jesus, wraps up His parable with this profound truth: "So will my heavenly Father do to you, unless each of you forgives his brother from his heart" (Mt 18:35). Yes, there are no limits to His mercy; however, if we don't show mercy, won't we receive the same treatment from our King that the unforgiving servant received from his king? Our King will *rescind* His mercy and forgiveness if we do not show others that same mercy, that same forgiveness, which we have received (*Note*[181]).

CHARITY AND MERCY

Parable Number 2: The Prodigal Son (Lk 15:11–32). Here, I would like to focus on an aspect of this parable that pertains to this particular study, namely the lavishness of the father's mercy. In this parable, the father is a depiction of God the Father. The parable thus conveys a sense of extravagance, overabundance, or, without offence, from a human perspective, may I dare even say, *wastefulness*, when it comes to God's mercy—God the Father is *prodigal* with His mercy.

I struggle with this over-the-top mercy. I am sure I am not the only one. Looking at the parable, if my son prematurely asked for his inheritance, then after squandering it, returned home, I would have a few choice words for him. By no means would I be killing a "fatted calf" and throwing a party for him. So, what's happening here? What we think is craziness is not craziness to God; what we might see as wastefulness is not wastefulness to God. Our logic is not God's logic (cf. Isa 55:7–9)—thankfully.

God is overgenerous with His mercy (Lk 15:20–24; also cf. Mt 20:14–15). In His Son, He wants all of us to return to Him. In fact, He is patiently looking and waiting for us to return to Him (Lk 15:20). He wants us to turn back to Him, to ask Him for His forgiveness and mercy. Even if we decide to turn to Him that is enough, for He is waiting to welcome us with His unconditional love. He is patiently waiting, like the father, to embrace us and to restore our dignity (Lk 15:22).

But do not forget our call to action. He wants each one of us (He even challenges us) to do the same. To be lavish with the mercy we show others. It is time for us to change our logic by learning "the meaning of the words, 'I desire mercy, not sacrifice'" (Mt 9:13; also cf. Isa 1:11–17 and Dan 3:38–41).

Parable Number 3: The Workers in the Vineyard (Mt 20:1–16). In this parable, the extravagant and generous landowner is also a depiction of God. Again, if it were up to me, I would not pay a full day's wages to someone who only worked an hour. Who would? It does not make any sense. From an economics or business point of view, this is pure craziness. Interesting to note, a similar parable is found within the rabbinic tradition,[182] but in that parable, the workers were paid extra, or a full day's wages, because they worked extra hard, so the landowner was impressed, thus compensated them accordingly. This I can understand. In Jesus' parable, however, this is not the case, as He clearly states that it is purely an overabundant generosity: "Am I not free to do as I wish with my own money? Are you envious because I am generous?" (Mt 20:15), the landowner asks.

That being said, another aspect in the parable deserves attention. In the role of the landowner, God shows mercy only to those who came at the end of the day, not to those who worked all day (Mt 20:14–16). This is an interesting point to ponder.

Some may now argue that the landowner showed mercy to those who worked all day by just hiring them. But is this mercy? Although work is good and work contributes to the dignity of the human person, giving work to the workers is not merciful in and of itself. Besides, Scripture tells us that "a worker's wage is credited not as a gift, but as something due" (Rom 4:4). The landowner did not show mercy on those hired earlier because he did not have to, for they already received a just wage as *something due* (Mt 20:13). He showed mercy on those hired later only because they required mercy, for not having received any work for the entire day; this extra pay was clearly a *gift* (Mt 20:15).

Again, work is good, and giving a person work and the ability to provide for their family is extremely good. But still, this is really not mercy. For when I hire a person, I hire that person because a job needs to be done, not because I show that person mercy. If not, we may also argue that the workers are merciful by working for the landowner in the high heat of noon. This is not the case. Hiring someone or working for someone is a *quid pro quo*. Hiring a person and paying them a just wage is justice, not mercy.

More to the point, the landowner could have easily shown mercy to those hired earlier by giving them a bonus or doubling their wages—an extra gift—for working in the dead heat; indeed, they were expecting it (Mt 20:10) and grumbled in disappointment when they did not get it (Mt 20:10-12).

Nevertheless, all said, from a theological point of view (i.e., seeing the vineyard as the Kingdom), and thus, viewing the parable as receiving work in the Kingdom, we can deduce that receiving work from the landowner is merciful, no matter what time of the day. Theologically speaking, there is no debate here, for we do not deserve to work in His Kingdom. It is not something we can earn. It is God, through His mercy, Who calls us and allows us to work in His Kingdom.

There is another point I would like to make. Giving the workers that came at the end of the day the same pay as the others might seem like the landowner is unfair with his compensation, or is devaluing the work of those who worked all day. This is so only if we forget, that a just wage was paid, and moreover, the theological meaning of the parable. Working in His Vineyard (His Kingdom) is a privilege and a gift. Again, it cannot be earned. There is no calculation here, and thus there is no devaluation.

Continuing with the theological note, if we truly *agape* (ἀγάπη) our neighbour (willing the good of our neighbour), then we will want our neighbour to have a full day's wage, so they can take care of their family. Also, again theologically speaking, we would want them to enter into the Kingdom of God. Therefore our grumbling is just that; it is grumbling, it is jealousy, it is envy, it is not *agape* (ἀγάπη).

Think about it from two points of view. First, by our grumbling, we are demonstrating our ungratefulness for our own calling, the gift, and the ability He has given us to work in His Kingdom. This is our grumbling. We see this within the older son (a depiction of the attitude of most Christians) in Parable Number 2 (Lk 15:29). If we were truly grateful, we would not be resentful of those who came at the end of the day or of the brother who returned after a life of partying (Lk 15:30). Second, if we truly *agape* (ἀγάπη) the other for their sake, we would want them to enter into the Kingdom of God. We would want to see their return. We would wish *all* to have a relationship with God.

Our inner attitude will demonstrate if the work we do toiling in the sun is a work of joy or grudging drudgery. It should be a work that we lovingly do for the *other*. Why? Because we *agape* (ἀγάπη) them; we should, therefore, want them to enter into that joy, in its fullness, even if they have just arrived at the last hour (Mt 20:6–7) or even if they have squandered their inheritance on a life of sinfulness (Lk 15:13; also cf. Lk 23:41–43).

True mercy—true *agape* (ἀγάπη)—will want even a Hitler, an Osama bin Laden, and so forth (despite all the atrocities they have committed), to enter the Kingdom of Heaven. We should not forget

WITNESS of CHARITY

that Jesus washed Judas' feet even though He foreknew Judas would betray Him (Jn 13:11).

———————

Having looked at the three parables, and keeping with our practical study, we will now highlight three different aspects of mercy:

Aspect Number 1: We will receive mercy in direct proportion to the mercy we give others. Mercy refrains from condemning or even judging others (an inherent tendency). Even if this judgment is justified, mercy refrains from giving the other this just judgment or condemnation. To put it another way, mercy is when we do not give the other the reproach they *justly* deserve. Why shouldn't we give others what they deserve? Because of Him who has shown His mercy to us and has refrained from giving us what we so *justly* deserve.

Yes, we can exercise *our* justice (judicial) if we so wish (Jn 8:5); however, as Jesus challenged the scribes and the Pharisees concerning the adulterous woman, He also challenges us (Jn 8:3–9). In recognition of our sinfulness, it is also best we refrain from casting that proverbial first stone (Jn 8:7). Yes, it is better to resolve our conflicts with mercy and forgiveness, rather than with justice (judicial). It is even better to leave justice (judicial) to God alone.

To an extent, we can use the distinctions that we used with the word *justice* to help us navigate the word *judgment*. For example, we can make the connection between justice (righteousness) and the just judgment of an act. We should strive for justice (righteousness) within ourselves and those around us. Conversely, justice (judicial) is more to do with the condemnation of the person. Even though we may exercise this justice (judicial), we are called to refrain (as previously mentioned in this chapter and in Chapter 3 Charity: It is Ethical and Moral).

To elaborate, God, out of *agape* (ἀγάπη) for us, shows us His mercy by not giving us what we so deserve. We are asked to do likewise: "Stop judging and you will not be judged, stop condemning and you will not be condemned" (Lk 6:37). The way we treat others will be the way we are treated (Mt 18:23ff; also cf. Sirach 28:1–4). The mercy we show others is the mercy we receive. God's conduct towards us is proportional to our conduct toward one another. Just think of the "Our Father" (the Lord's Prayer). Don't we ask to be forgiven in direct proportion to the way we forgive others? Some may question if it is a "direct proportion" or "in the manner of." I think we are splitting hairs here; therefore, for argument's sake, we could say it is both. For "as we judge, so will we be judged, and the measure with which we measure will be measured out to us" (Mt 7:2), and as we forgive, we will be forgiven (Lk 6:37). "So speak and so act as people who will be judged by the law of freedom; for the judgment is merciless to one who has not shown mercy; mercy triumphs over judgment" (Jms 2:12–13).

Aspect Number 2: Only by the grace of God (1 Cor 15:10). In showing others mercy, there is the recognition that in our own human frailty, we do not know how we would react under different circumstances, trials, and tribulations. If we were in a similar situation as they, would we do the same? Or would we do something even worse? Therefore, we refrain from the judgment (condemnation) of another person, for we do not know how we would react in that particular circumstance. As talked about, this is not a prohibition against recognizing a sinful act or faulty human behaviour, but it is about passing judgment on the *person*, in arrogance, and disregarding our faults and sinfulness (cf. Mt 7:3–5 and Lk 6:39). Our judgment becomes poor judgment, for we are not all knowing, and we judge by appearances (Jn 7:24). Therefore, in our judgment of the *person*, we become hypocritical (Mt 7:5). By moving our judgment beyond the *act* itself, by judging or condemning the *person* and assuming a position on the judgment seat, we are assuming we are in the place of God (Heb 10:30; also cf. Rom 12:19).

Remember, we "all have sinned and are deprived of the glory of God" (Rom 3:23). We all are undeservedly justified by God's freely given gift of grace "through the redemptive work in Christ Jesus" (Rom 3:24). This is how God manifested His justice (Rom 3:25–26). Therefore, it is only through the grace of God that we move forward. So, who are we to judge the soul of our brothers and sisters? Who are we to assume the judgment seat?

To elaborate, I remember that during a prison ministry in a US women's correctional facility, I met a young woman who, as a young

WITNESS OF CHARITY

child, was forced to sleep on the floor next to her mother's bed, while her mother entertained different men while she slept. This lasted for about four years until she was twelve, when one of her mother's consorts abused her.

If you were this girl, how would you react? How would this experience change your life? Well, she ran away and got involved with so-called boyfriends who also abused her. She told me a story of one boyfriend who sold her for a pack of cigarettes and another who sold her for a bottle of booze. Eventually, at age eighteen, she ended up in prison. When I met her, she was about nineteen years old. I do not remember why she was in prison—let us assume the courts were justified in their punishment—nonetheless, would you *condemn her*, as a person? How would we react to similar situations? If our life circumstances were different, would we be in her shoes?

Please do not mistake not condemning her as letting her go free without consequence. She, and only she, is responsible for her actions. Justice (judicial) must be served in one form or another, as we shall see in Aspect Number 3. Yes, she should remain in prison. Here, however, is the paradox: we do not *condemn her* or others like her, but we do not open the penitentiaries and let people go free.

May I suggest that it is in this paradox that Jesus asks us to visit those in prison? Not because they are not guilty (again, for argument's sake, let us assume that they are), but it is because we should not condemn them as people. We should not make a judgment on the person; we should not judge their inner intention for we do not know their circumstances.

Having said that, maybe there is another reason. Just maybe, it is a reminder or a realization to those who are not in prison that it is only through the grace of God that we are not (*Note*[183]). Yes, it is "but by the grace of God I am what I am" (1 Cor 15:10). We are not in prison only by His grace—humbling, isn't it?

Aspect Number 3: Mercy does not usurp justice. As affirmed, mercy does not abrogate justice (judicial). How then, do we reconcile mercy and justice (judicial)? Remember that in Chapter 5, Charity and the Law, we looked at the word *fulfill*, in Greek, πληρόω (plēroō/play-ro'-o). At that point, I pointed out that there are two predominant definitions of this word. There, we looked at the first definition (the eschatological sense); here, I would like to look at the second definition, for it gives insight into the connection between God's mercy and justice (judicial). To recall, the second definition of *plēroō* (πληρόω),means to complete, carry out through to the end, render perfect, bring to pass, ratify, or accomplish.

Keeping this second definition in mind—and strictly from Jesus' point of view and not that of the accusers (i.e., the scribes and the Pharisees)—we will briefly look at the story of the adulterous woman (Jn 8:3–11) by using three steps, which, in addition, will also help us understand the basic mechanics of atonement, righteousness, and justification (*Note*[184]).

In this Gospel narrative, Jesus is the only One remaining (Jn 8:10) because He is the only One without sin (Jn 8:7). Thus, at this point, based on His own criteria (Jn 8:7), He may justly stone her. Nevertheless, Jesus does not justly condemn her (cf. Lk 23:41), or put her to death as prescribed by the law (Lev 20:10 and Deut 22:22), but He releases her. This action on Jesus' part, however, does not usurp the law. Why? For as we have seen, not only is He the actual writer of the law, He is also the fulfillment of the law. Therefore, He well knows that justice (judicial) must be fulfilled, which means that justice (judicial) demands payment (i.e., Step 1—atonement). Here now is where the second definition of the word *plēroō* (πληρόω) comes into play.

Jesus, within Himself, *fulfills* (completes, carries out through to the end, renders perfect, brings to pass, ratifies, and accomplishes) the law's requirements (i.e., Step 2—righteousness), which is imputed to the adulterous women (*Note*[185]). He Himself *fulfills* the law's literal requirements in Himself. He makes the *payment* that justice (judicial) demands, and it is only because of His loving action (purely the grace of God), that He allows the adulterous woman to go free (i.e., Step 3—justification).

Now, some of you may be thinking how this could be. This event takes place before Jesus' actual crucifixion. However, the efficacy of the crucifixion is not dependent on its time in our history. Christ's death was sufficient for the forgiveness of sins (and payment for sins) for all time. Also keep in mind, that in Saint John's Gospel, Jesus is well aware of His imminent crucifixion (cf. Jn 2:19–22, 11:25, 12:24, 12:33, and 18:32).

Interestingly, the Gospel of Saint John even takes it a step further by framing this particular event with the crucifixion in sight, by referring to the Mount of Olives (Jn 8:1), which is not referred to anywhere else in this Gospel, or outside of the Passion week in any of the other three Gospels. Justice (judicial) demands payment—Jesus knows that. Jesus does not usurp the law—the Gospel writers knows that (*Note*[186]). Therefore *yes*, Jesus *pays* her penalty of being put to death. He takes it on and makes payment for it; by atoning for it on the cross, and thus fulfilling the law's requirements, making her righteous, and for her justification, God raised Him up (Rom 4:25).

Briefly, God, in Jesus, demonstrates His justice (judicial), precisely through justice (righteousness), through His mercy. Mercy has not nullified justice (judicial). Also, keep in mind, that both justice (judicial) and justice (righteousness) are rooted in *agape* (ἀγάπη). Nevertheless, justice (righteousness) surpasses and fulfills justice (judicial). It transcends it and converts it.

In this narrative—and by extension as it affects you and me—Jesus, in His mercy, has taken on our penalty; He has taken on *our* judgment; He has taken on *our* prison time; He has paid *our* debt in full; thus fulfilling the demands of the law (*Note*[187]). Because of that, He is not unjust in dispensing His justice (righteousness) for He has fulfilled the legal requirements the law demands (e.g., being stoned to death). It is for that reason that Saint Paul says, "Do not nullify the grace of God, for if justification comes through the law, then Christ died for nothing" (Gal 2:21; also cf. Rom 5:21).

On this note, it is essential that we *not* take His mercy for granted, or we might face His justice (judicial). Remember the statement "He can show mercy to whomever He wishes." Well, to reiterate (for this should be underscored), He can show us His justice (judicial) or His justice (righteousness), as He wishes without being arbitrary or capricious. As talked about in Parable Number 3, The Workers in the Vineyard (and stated arguments notwithstanding), He showed His justice (judicial) to those who worked all day (Mt 20:4 and 20:13), and His justice (righteousness) to those who came at the end of the day (Mt 20:14–16; also cf. Ex 33:19). Keep that in mind.

To elaborate, let us look at two things we are called to do. First, by helping our neighbours to see the wrong they have done, we lead them to the path of forgiveness (without forgiveness, we cannot speak

CHARITY AND MERCY

of any form of justice) and then ultimately to their receiving divine mercy.

Second, we are called to take on the penalty that the other deserves. This is the tough one, but remember, "no one has greater love than this, to lay down one's life for one's friends" (Jn 15:13). We must take on the death, the penalty that our neighbour or our enemy justly deserves, and lay down our life, just as Jesus did with the adulterous woman. Now you know why I said that I struggle with this concept of mercy, for it is far from easy. However, as we go through this personal struggle, we realize that it is only through the grace of God that this is possible (*Note*[188]).

On the lighter side, and to get this point across, I am reminded of a story I once heard during a homily. It goes something like this: Little Johnny was a rambunctious, energetic little boy. After school, he would go out to play with his friends. With him, time would always wander, so he would repeatedly come home late for dinner. Despite many warnings from his parents, little Johnny pressed the limit. One day, little Johnny's parents warned him by saying, "Next time you are late for dinner, all you'll receive is one slice of bread and a glass of water." Little Johnny loved food, so his parents hoped that this expected punishment would work.

The next day, as usual, little Johnny went out to play. Fifteen minutes before dinner, little Johnny's mother called out for him through the kitchen window. Hearing his mother's call, little Johnny thought, "Just a few minutes more." A few minutes became more than a few minutes; again, little Johnny was late for dinner. As little Johnny entered the dining room, there was silence. His mother had cooked all of little Johnny's favourite foods. The aroma was in the air, and his little stomach was churning; but at his place setting, there was only one slice of bread and a glass of water. Little Johnny sat down quietly, stared at his one slice of bread, and then lowering his face; he looked down and sat motionlessly. A single tear rolled down his little cheek. After about five minutes, little Johnny's father picked up little Johnny's plate and switched it with his. His father took on his son's penalty and traded places with his son. Little Johnny's father then ate the one slice of bread and drank the glass of water. He told his son to eat all his favourite food now placed in front of him. After that day, little Johnny was never late for dinner.

The father did not dismiss little Johnny's punishment. Parents that are reading this know what happens when they give in to their children and do not follow through with their just punishments. Without law, there will only be chaos. Remember, justice must be served one way or another, for it is the loving thing to do. Here, justice was served, through the mercy of little Johnny's father; he held to justice, but through mercy, which gave little Johnny a powerful lesson.

Let us end this chapter with two separate texts that summarize what we have discussed and give us some added insight. The first text is a sermon from Saint Caesarius of Arles, a bishop from the early sixth century:

> *Blessed are the merciful, for they shall receive mercy.* My brothers and sisters, sweet is the thought of mercy, but even more so is mercy itself. It is what all men hope for, but unfortunately, not what all men deserve. For while all men wish to receive it, only a few are willing to give it. How can a man ask for himself what he refuses to give to another? If he expects to receive any mercy in heaven, he should give mercy on earth. Do we all desire to receive mercy? Let us make mercy our patroness now, and she will free us in the world to come.
> There is an earthly as well as heavenly mercy, that is to say, a human and a divine mercy. Human mercy has love on the miseries of the poor. Divine mercy grants forgiveness of sins. Whatever human mercy bestows here on earth, divine mercy will return to us in our homeland. Yes, God who sees fit to give His mercy in heaven wishes it to be a reality here on earth.
> What kind of people are we? When God gives, we wish to receive, but when He begs, we refuse to give. What do you wish for, what do you pray for, my dear

brothers and sisters, when you come to church? Is it mercy? How can it be anything else? Show mercy, then, while you are on earth, and mercy will be shown to you in heaven.[189]

| Saint Caesarius of Arles |

For the following text, I placed together a few paragraphs from the Papal Bull of Indiction,[190] *Misericordiae Vultus* (*MV*), which promulgated the Extraordinary Jubilee of Mercy:

Jesus Christ is the face of the Father's mercy. These words might well sum up the mystery of the Christian faith. Mercy has become living and visible in Jesus of Nazareth, reaching its culmination in Him. The Father, "rich in mercy" (Eph 2:4), after having revealed His name to Moses as "a God merciful and gracious, slow to anger, and abounding in steadfast love and faithfulness" (Ex 34:6), has never ceased to show, in various ways throughout history, His divine nature. In the "fullness of time" (Gal 4:4), when everything had been arranged according to His plan of salvation, He sent His only Son into the world, born of the Virgin Mary, to reveal His love for us in a definitive way. Whoever sees Jesus sees the Father (cf. Jn 14:9). Jesus of Nazareth, by His words, His actions, and His entire Person reveals the mercy of God. (*MV* 1)
We need constantly to contemplate the mystery of mercy. It is a wellspring of joy, serenity, and peace. Our salvation depends on it. Mercy: the word reveals the very mystery of the Most Holy Trinity. Mercy: the ultimate and supreme act by which God comes to meet us. Mercy: the fundamental law that dwells in the heart of every person who looks sincerely into the eyes of his brothers and sisters on the path of life. Mercy: the bridge that connects God and man, opening our hearts to the hope of being loved forever despite our sinfulness. (*MV* 2)

Mercy will always be greater than any sin, and no one can place limits on the love of God who is ever ready to forgive. (*MV* 3)

We recall the poignant words of Saint John XXIII when, opening the Council, he indicated the path to follow: "Now the Bride of Christ wishes to use the medicine of mercy rather than taking up arms of severity . . . the Catholic Church, as She holds high the torch of Catholic truth at this Ecumenical Council, wants to show Herself a loving mother to all; patient, kind, moved by compassion and goodness toward Her separated children." Blessed Paul VI spoke in a similar vein at the closing of the Council: "We prefer to point out how charity has been the principal religious feature of this Council . . . the old story of the Good Samaritan has been the model of the spirituality of the Council . . . a wave of affection and admiration flowed from the Council over the modern world of humanity. Errors were condemned, indeed, because charity demanded this no less than did truth, but for individuals themselves there was only admonition, respect and love." (*MV* 4)

The Church's first truth is the love of Christ. The Church makes Herself a servant of this love and mediates it to all people: a love that forgives and expresses itself in the gift of oneself. (*MV* 12)

In order to be capable of mercy, therefore, we must first of all dispose ourselves to listen to the Word of God. This means rediscovering the value of silence in order to meditate on the Word that comes to us. (*MV* 13)

In mercy, we find proof of how God loves us. He gives his entire self, always, freely, asking nothing in return. (*MV* 14)

It would not be out of place at this point to recall the relationship between *justice* [judicial] and *mercy*. These are not two contradictory realities, but two dimensions of a single reality that unfolds progressively until it culminates in the fullness of love.

CHARITY AND MERCY

Justice [judicial] is a fundamental concept for civil society, which is meant to be governed by the rule of law. Justice [judicial] is also understood as that which is rightly due to each individual. In the Bible, there are many references to divine justice [judicial] and to God as "judge." In these passages, justice [judicial] is understood as the full observance of the Law and the behaviour of every good Israelite in conformity with God's commandments. Such a vision, however, has frequently led to legalism by distorting the original meaning of justice [judicial and righteousness] and obscuring its profound value. To overcome this legalistic perspective, we need to recall that in Sacred Scripture, justice [righteousness] is conceived essentially as the faithful abandonment of oneself to God's will. (*MV* 20)

Mercy is not opposed to justice [judicial] but rather expresses God's way of reaching out to the sinner, offering him a new chance to look at himself, convert, and believe . . . If God limited Himself to only justice [judicial], He would cease to be God, and would instead be like human beings who ask merely that the law be respected. But mere justice [judicial] is not enough. Experience shows that an appeal to justice [judicial] alone will result in its destruction. This is why God goes beyond justice [judicial] with His mercy and forgiveness [justice (righteousness)]. Yet this does not mean that justice [judicial] should be devalued or rendered superfluous. On the contrary: anyone who makes a mistake must pay the price. However, this is just the beginning of conversion, not its end, because one begins to feel the tenderness and mercy of God. God does not deny justice [judicial]. He rather envelopes it and surpasses it with an even greater event in which we experience [*agape* (ἀγάπη)] as the foundation of true justice [judicial and righteousness]. (*MV* 21)[191]

| *Misericordiae Vultus* |

God is *agape* (ἀγάπη).
Therefore, our love is rooted in Him.

Chapter 8 | Charity: The Ultimate Source

"God is *agape* (ἀγάπη)" (1 Jn 4:16). We have now reached the pinnacle of this study.

For the sake of clarity (just as we did with mercy), we can compartmentalize this statement—God is *agape* (ἀγάπη)—into two parts, making it easier to study. The first has more to do with our understanding of God Himself. That is the movement of love within the Godhead.[192] The second has to do with God's love for His creation. His love, in essence, also initiates a threefold movement of love: first, from God to creation; second, from creation to creation; and third, from creation back to God.

For the first part, we must understand that God *is agape* (ἀγάπη)—period. His love is absolute. Unlike what we discovered with mercy, this declaration—God *is agape* (ἀγάπη)—has nothing to do with us, as created beings (or creation). God's *agape* (ἀγάπη) is absolute and thus existed long before creation, within the Godhead.

However, it was only fully shown to *us* through the revelation of Christ Jesus. In the Person of Jesus, the apostles received great insight, which enabled them to make two earth-shattering declarations. The first comes from Saint Thomas who, when confronted with the resurrected Christ, boldly declares, "My Lord and my God" (Jn 20:28). Today, in Christian circles, we might take this pronouncement for granted. It is hard for us as Gentile Christians to grasp the implications of this declaration fully. For a first-century Jew, however, even to think it would be a blasphemy. That said, fascinatingly, as a first-century Jew, Saint Thomas makes such a startling assertion. Despite our brainpower (or Saint Thomas'), we cannot *comprehend* totally this new reality (or a better word would be *mystery*); nonetheless, we can *apprehend* it.

The second earth-shattering declaration comes from Saint John, who boldly proclaims, "God is *agape* (ἀγάπη)" (1 Jn 4:16). So, why is this earth shattering? Well, there are implications to this statement, which again, as Gentile Christians we might take for granted. Let me explain. We state God *is agape* (ἀγάπη). Love, to be authentic, needs both a *subject* and an *object* (a lover and a beloved); if not, it would cease to be *agape* (ἀγάπη), for it would be self-centred, i.e., self-love. God is the subject of love; therefore, who's the object of love? There are only two options. The first option is creation. However, if the object of love is creation, we must conclude that God would not have been *agape* (ἀγάπη) prior to creation, unless creation was eternal like He is. This option is scientifically, philosophically, and theologically contradictory (for all three disciplines consider the world to be finite). The second option is that the object of love *is* God Himself. If this were correct, it might be construed as self-love; this is why the Old Testament does not make the declaration that God *is* love until the understanding of a triune God was revealed in the New Testament.

Within the Trinity, within the unity of One God, *love* is expressed and received by each of the three Persons (God the Father, God the Son, and God the Holy Spirit). *Love*, therefore, *is* the grounds for the claim that God is a trinity of Persons; and vice versa, the claim that God is a trinity of Persons is the basis for the declaration that "God is *agape* (ἀγάπη)" (1 Jn 4:16). This cannot be said with a unitarian view of God.

In other words, in light of the Trinity, we can legitimately declare that God *is agape* (ἀγάπη). He is the ultimate source of love, and thus He causes all love. Keeping this in mind, the word *Trinity* is only a word that describes this reality. The word *Trinity* is not found in the Bible, but it was used by the Early Church, among other words (e.g., *Hypostaseis, Ousia, Persona*), to help us apprehend the mystery of the Godhead, the reality of a triune God, the revelation of God that corresponds to the truth found in the Bible (cf. Jn 1:8, 14:9, and 15:26), which was ultimately revealed through Christ Jesus (which we are unable to comprehend totally), nevertheless, it is only because of this revelation in Christ that Saint John could proclaim, "God is *agape* (ἀγάπη)" (1 Jn 4:16). God can only be *agape* (ἀγάπη) if God is trinitarian; if not, God would need creation or would be caught up in self-love (*Note*[193]).

I want to make two additional points before we move on to the second part. First, God *is* love; however, let us not mistakenly think that love is *God*. Despite this notion being presented to us by various Eastern religions and the New Age movement, love is *not* God. God *is God*! Since God is self-existent, God *is God* from all eternity, and as deduced God *is agape* (ἀγάπη) from all eternity.

WITNESS of CHARITY

Second, as mentioned in the previous chapter, there is no such thing as an Old Testament God and a New Testament God. If you believe in this notion of a fire-and-brimstone God of the Old Testament versus a kinder, gentler, loving God of the New Testament, you are theologically misinformed. God is *God*—and He is unchangeable (Rev 22:13 and Heb 13:8). Sacred Scripture, however, presents a gradual unfolding or revealing of God, through a progressive course of action in dealing with His creation, through time (also known as Salvation History[194]).

Here is a simple analogy that might help. When we were babies or toddlers, our parents instructed us mainly in the negative, for example, "Don't do this," "Don't do that." As we grew and our understanding increased, we were now also punished for doing what we were told not to do; but our parents only gave us a rationale to the limit of our understanding. The older we became, the increasingly sophisticated the explanation became—akin to the change we see between the Old Testament and the New Testament. In the Old Testament, we see Israel as an infant, a toddler, an adolescent, and a teenager. As we move into the New Testament, Israel becomes a young adult, and eventually, the Church was seen—and was dealt with—as an adult. Therefore, the ultimate revelation in Jesus the Christ, and the meaning and consequences of this revelation (i.e., the "why"), could be taught through the writings that became the New Testament.

As I state in Appendix A, what we have is a gradual revealing of the mystery of the Trinity, which was present from *all* eternity, the God who

> ➤ presented Himself to Abraham (Gen 12:1, 14:18, and 18:1–15)—i.e., the infant years;
> ➤ declared Himself to Moses as subsistent Being, *Ipsum Esse*,[195] the Great "I AM WHO I AM" (Ex 3:14), in Hebrew אֶהְיֶה אֲשֶׁר אֶהְיֶה (*Ehyeh Aser Ehyeh*), in Greek ἐγώ εἰμί (*Ego Eimi*) "I EXIST"—not a being among beings, but the sheer act of Being Itself, *Ipsum Esse* ("to be")—i.e., the toddler and adolescent years, and eventually teenage years; and,

CHARITY: THE ULTIMATE SOURCE

➤ in the fullness of time, revealed Himself in Christ Jesus (Gal 4:4)—i.e., the young adult and adult years.

Yes, this God—who is One God, who is Truth itself, who is Love itself—over time revealed Himself in three Persons: "God the Father," "God the Son," and "God the Holy Spirit" (*CCC* #253–255). I encourage you to read and reread, contemplate and meditate, upon the words of Saint Athanasius found in Appendix A.

Now, we can unequivocally conclude that the first part of stating that God *is agape* (ἀγάπη) is clearly a reference within the Trinity— that God *is agape* (ἀγάπη), period. We can now move to the second part.

Here we must acknowledge the fact that God need not create (to have something or someone to love, as we deduced). Therefore, we can state that He has no reason to create—for God is *complete* within Himself. We can consequently further conclude that God creates because He *wants* to, moreover, because of His *agape* (ἀγάπη) for humanity (*Note*[196]). In addition, the angels and the cosmos were all created, not out of a *need* that God has to fulfill, but purely out of *agape* (ἀγάπη). He creates because of His overabundant love; there is no other explanation. We may argue that even hell[197] was created because of His total love for us. Due to the vastness of His love for us, He not only sends His Son to become a creature like us, but He also allows His Son to die on a cross for us so we, the creature, may have eternal life with Him, the Creator.

The fact that God creates us (humanity) totally out of love also initiates a threefold movement of love. Again, first is a movement of love from God to His creation. Second is a movement of love from creation to creation. Third is a movement of love (a reciprocation of His love) from us, His creation, back to Him. Unfortunately, the second and third movements are not always a given (which is another discussion). That said, however, as Christians, to love God (this reciprocal love for the love He has shown us), we must *decide* to follow Him and to do His will (*Note*[198]). In which, there is a fundamental call to love our neighbour (second movement). For this is primary in the movement of love from the creature back to the Creator (third movement). "Whoever hates his brother is in darkness;

WITNESS OF CHARITY

he walks in darkness and does not know where he is going" (1 Jn 2:11), for those who say,

> "I love God," and hate their neighbour, are liars; for those who do not love a brother or sister whom they have seen, cannot love God whom they have not seen. The commandment we have from Him is this: those who love God must also love their neighbour. (1 Jn 4:20–21)[199]

This addresses the problem we face, for

> we cannot be sure if we are loving God, although we may have good reasons for believing that we are; but we can know quite well if we are loving our neighbour. And be certain that, the farther advanced you find you are in this, the greater the love you will have for God.[200]
>
> | Saint Teresa of Avila |

Yes, on our part, this is the only proper response to His love (cf. 1 Jn 4:7–8 and Lk 19:8). For in our neighbour, we see and find Jesus; and through Jesus, we see and find the Trinity. Keep in mind however, that this movement is only possible and attainable because of Him who first loved us; we love, and must love "because He first loved us" (1 Jn 4:19).

We now have the culmination of everything discussed in this study. Here is the crescendo . . .

> God is [agape (ἀγάπη)], and whoever remains in love remains in God and God in him . . . We have come to know and to believe in the love God has for us. (1 Jn 4:16)

For God so loved the world that He gave His only
Son, so that everyone who believes in Him might not
perish but might have eternal life. (Jn 3:16)
Therefore, brothers and sisters let us love one
another, because love is of God; everyone who loves
is begotten by God and knows God. Whoever is
without love does not know God, for God is [agape
(ἀγάπη)]. In this way the love of God was revealed to
us: God sent His only Son into the world so that we
might have life through Him. In this is love: not that
we have loved God, but that He loved us and sent His
Son as expiation for our sins. Beloved, if God so
loved us, we also must love one another. No one has
ever seen God. Yet if we love one another, God
remains in us, and His [agape (ἀγάπη)] is brought to
perfection in us. (1 Jn 4:7–12)

With this, we can now see the significance of the primary
image—of Christ crucified. The *beams* of the cross of Christ provide
us with a powerful image upon which to meditate. In this context, the
vertical *beam*, which points towards the heavens, speaks of the love
of God—encompassing the first three commandments. The horizontal
beam, which not only speaks of the love of neighbour—
encompassing the last seven commandments—but also, and more
importantly, speaks of the span of Christ's love for all humanity.

"God is *agape* (ἀγάπη)" Saint John the Apostle boldly
proclaims! Is there a better love than this? We have heard these words
many times. The risk we run is that we take this love for granted.
Please do not make this just a footnote. Do not take it for granted;
read and reread, and most of all, contemplate what Saint John is
telling us. With this declaration, with this image, we have been given
a great insight that should be reflected upon, meditated upon,
internalized, and most importantly, lived.

In his first encyclical as Pope, *Deus Caritas Est* (*God is Love*)
(*DCE*) Benedict XVI wanted to affirm and remind us of this. Here I
would like to summarize Pope Benedict XVI's thought, using his
powerful words and insight:

This is love in its most radical form. By contemplating the pierced side of Christ (cf. Jn 19:37), we can understand the starting point of: "God is [agape (ἀγάπη)]" (1 Jn 4:8). It is there that this truth can be contemplated. It is from there that our definition of love must begin. (*DCE* 12)

Union with Christ is also union with all those to whom He gives Himself. I cannot possess Christ just for myself; I can belong to Him only in union with all those who have become, or who will become, His own. We become "one body," completely joined in a single existence. Love of God and love of neighbour are now truly united. (*DCE* 14)

Faith, worship, and *ethos* are interwoven as a single reality . . . "Worship" itself, Eucharistic communion, includes the reality both of being loved and of loving others in turn. Love of God and love of neighbour have become one. One is so closely connected to the other that to say that we love God becomes a lie if we are closed to our neighbour or hate him altogether. (*DCE* 14, 15, and 16)

True, no one has ever seen God as He is. And yet God is not totally invisible to us; He does not remain completely inaccessible . . . this love of God has appeared in our midst . . . God has made Himself visible: in Jesus we are able to see the Father (cf. Jn 14:9). (*DCE* 17)

Love of neighbour is thus shown to be possible in the way proclaimed by the Bible, by Jesus. It consists in the very fact that, in God and with God, I love even the person whom I do not like or even know . . . I learn to look on this other person not simply with my eyes and my feelings, but from the perspective of Jesus Christ. His friend is my friend. Love [agape (ἀγάπη)] is "divine" because it comes from God and unites us to God. "If you see charity [agape (ἀγάπη)], you see the Trinity." (*DCE* 18 and 19)[201]

| Pope Benedict XVI |

Conclusion

As stated, in the title, *Witness of Charity*, I have deliberately used the word *of* instead of *to*. Depending on how we comprehend and internalize this will make a difference in our disposition and worldview. For we are not merely a witness *to* someone. We are a witness *of* Someone. Let me repeat: as Christians, we are not merely witnesses *to* charity or witnesses *to* Christ, but we are witnesses *of* Christ (Note[202]).

He is not Someone outside of us or external to us. No, He is within us. Therefore we are witnesses *of* Him; we operate for Him, the One Whom we have heard, Whom we have seen with our eyes, Whom we have gazed upon and touched with our hands, Whom we have tasted and have internalized (cf. 1 Jn 1:1, Mt 26:26–27, Jn 6:55–57, and Mt 28:19–20). We are literally His hands, His feet, and His body.

Consequently, there is a *twist* to the three images that I have proposed at the beginning of this study. The twist is that we become Christ Jesus in each of these three images. We become Christ and as *servant* as we wash our neighbour's feet. We become Christ when we become that *Good Samaritan* to our neighbour. And most importantly, we become Christ on the *cross* when we lay down our life for our neighbour and our enemy.

Yes! This is the *new commandment* in Christ Jesus. We are called to love our neighbour as *He* loves (Jn 13:34 and Jn 15:12). Every day that our Lord has given us is a day to *agape* (ἀγάπη) our neighbour and our enemy. We are all created in the image and likeness of God (Gen 1:26; also cf. 5:3) therefore we must love and respect each other in His image. This starts by always recognizing His *agape* (ἀγάπη) for us. The *law* states that "you shall love the LORD, your God, with all your heart, and with all your soul, and with all your strength" (Deut 6:5). However, the fulfillment of this law is "not that we have loved God, but that He loved us" (1 Jn 4:10; also cf. 1 Jn 4:7–21). Our motivation is prompted by God's *agape* (ἀγάπη) for us.

We must therefore *rest* in His *agape* (ἀγάπη) for us. It is only then that we can *agape* (ἀγάπη) Him with the totality of our being

(*Note*[203]), and *agape* (ἀγάπη) our neighbour and enemy in Him. Therefore, seriously contemplate the love He shows us (cf. Jn 3:16, Rom 5:8, and Eph 2:4–5). Then rejoice in that love. Rejoice that He cares for us. Rejoice that He has mercy for us. Rejoice that He has blotted out our transgressions and taken away our sins. As Saint Paul boldly proclaims: "Rejoice in the Lord always. I shall say it again: Rejoice!" (Phil 4:4).

Saint Paul also tells us that nothing—absolutely nothing—can separate us from the love of Christ (Rom 8:35). Not "anguish, or distress, or persecution, or famine, or nakedness, or peril, or the sword" (Rom 8:35); he is also absolutely convinced that "neither death, nor life, nor angels, nor principalities, nor present things, nor future things, nor powers, nor height, nor depth, nor any other creature will be able to separate us from the love of God in Christ Jesus our Lord" (Rom 8:38–39). For that reason, nothing—absolutely nothing—should separate us from the love we show each other, our neighbour, and our enemy. Not even if they hurt us, or persecute us, or condemn us, or slander us, or terrorize us, or cause all kinds of grief to us, nothing should separate us from our *agape* (ἀγάπη) for each other.

This is our joyful pursuit, our joy-filled reaction to the joy of Him Who shows His *agape* (ἀγάπη) for us. Therefore we must go and, in sincerity and without hypocrisy (in return for His love), *agape* (ἀγάπη) one another, our neighbour and our enemy—in Truth!

In closing, always keep in mind that we must first allow ourselves to receive His *agape* (ἀγάπη) because we cannot *agape* (ἀγάπη) without Him. Yes, we love and must love with extraordinary Christian *agape* (ἀγάπη) because of His love for us.

Faith ends, for it will eventually yield to sight; hope ends, for it will eventually yield to possession; but love—*agape* (ἀγάπη)—never ends; it will remain and endure for all eternity (1 Cor 13:13), for God is *agape* (ἀγάπη). PERIOD. Therefore, in the words of Saint Paul:

> Let love be sincere; hate what is evil, hold on to what is good; love one another with brotherly love . . . Do not grow slack in zeal, be fervent in spirit, serve the Lord. Rejoice in hope, endure in affliction, persevere in prayer . . . Bless those who persecute

(you), bless and do not curse them. Rejoice with those who rejoice, weep with those who weep. Have the same regard for one another; do not be haughty but associate with the lowly; do not be wise in your own estimation. Do not repay anyone evil for evil; be concerned for what is noble in the sight of all. If possible, on your part, live at peace with all.
My brothers and sisters, do not look for revenge . . . rather, "if your enemy is hungry, feed him; if he is thirsty, give him something to drink" . . . Do not be conquered by evil but conquer evil with good. (Rom 12:9–21)

Let us pray:
Almighty and Merciful God,
You break the power of evil and make all things new
in Your Son Jesus the Messiah, the King of the universe.
We ask that You fill Your Church with the spirit of AGAPE (ἀγάπη).
Teach us to AGAPE (ἀγάπη) You in our neighbour,
and in serving them to serve You.
On the Cross You asked pardon for Your executioners,
teach us to AGAPE (ἀγάπη) our enemies
and pray for those who persecute us.
May Your Spirit give us the courage
and make us strong and willing
to offer our lives for the good of our neighbour and our enemies.
We ask this through our Lord Jesus the Messiah, Your Son,
who lives and reigns with You and the Holy Spirit,
All Holy, All Glorious, All Precious, All Beautiful, All Powerful,
All Knowing, All Good, All Merciful
and All Loving God for ages unending
Amen.[204]

Appendix A | Methodology and Presuppositions

Too many Christian academics, teachers, preachers, and priests believe theology should be relegated only to "theologians" or scholars. They state that theology should not be taught or preached to the average Christian in the pew. That ordinary Christians should only concern themselves with ritual or pious religious practices, and should not trouble themselves with theological issues that are "beyond" them. More than a few Christians, maybe even some reading this, may also agree with the above view. We might say: "I don't have time for theology. I'm not a priest. Besides, I'm also okay with my current understanding of Christianity."

I, however, do not agree with either view. I do not agree with the condescending "there-there" mentality on the one side or with the "indifference to theology works for me" on the other side. On the contrary, I agree with those who believe that *all* Christians should be theologians. Why? The fact that we believe in God and profess our Creed should make us theologians.

Let me explain. The English word *theology* comes from the Greek word θεολογία (theologia/*thē-ə-'lō-ja*), which derives from two Greek words Θεός (Theos/*Theós*), meaning God, and λογία (logia/*'lo.gi.a*), a Greek word rooted in the word λόγος (logos/*log'-os*), meaning a word, a rational cause, an account, a teaching, or reason. Simply put, then, theology is reasoning or the study about God. As Christians, we must agree that ignorance of God is *not* an option. As a result, we must *study* God so we may have a mature understanding of who God *is*. This necessary study—by default—automatically makes us theologians.

This book is designed to help us with this study about God, by conveying fundamental theological truths concerning *Christian charity*, with simplicity and clarity, so we may grow in our knowledge of God in this particular area. Moreover, as with any study, it calls us to personal change.

In the words of Saint Teresa of Calcutta, "We must know the faith well, love the faith, and live the faith: know, love, and live."[205] This assertion has three parts:

1. Know: The study of God is not merely an academic exercise or an education in isolation. The study's theological truths are practical; thus, they must become the *foundation* upon which we stand.
2. Love: The study of God must consume us. We must *love* this study, for there is nothing more significant than wholly occupying our minds and our hearts, and entirely focusing our attention on everything that is God (Mk 12:30 and Deut 6:5).
3. Live: The study of God must consequently *change* us, our character and our lifestyle, so that we may live a joy-filled and mature Christian life.

I hope and pray you agree with this.

To borrow from Saint Paul (1 Cor 13:11), when we were babies, we ate baby food. As we grew up, however, were we still content to eat baby food? Or, did we desire something of greater sustenance? Well then, it is time we put aside our childish ways (1 Cor 13:11), and embark upon this necessary study of God, so we may *know* Him, *love* Him, and *live* in Him.

As the story goes, Vince Lombardi, the former head coach of the Green Bay Packers (1959–1967), would begin every football season by bringing all the players into the locker room, raising the football, and saying: "Gentlemen, this is a *football!*" Even though some players had multiple Super Bowl rings, and some had lived and breathed football since childhood, he would start every season in the same manner. Some players might be annoyed at the banality or obviousness of this statement; however, this back-to-the-basics mentality garnered him an unsurpassed reputation in the world of football.

I share this story because the approach of this book is the same. Obviousness acknowledged, I am also taking this back-to-the-basics approach in this study. Consequently, I hold up this book and say, "Ladies and gentlemen, this is *Christian charity!*" With that

APPENDIX A

understanding, here is my *Methodology and Presuppositions*, which I have divided into twelve key areas:

1. God: When I use the word *God*, I am referring to the *Mystery of the Trinity*, the One Who presented Himself to Abraham (Gen 12:1); Who declared Himself to Moses, as subsistent Being (*Ipsum Esse*), the Great "I AM WHO I AM" (Ex 3:14)—in Hebrew אֲשֶׁר אֶהְיֶה אֶהְיֶה (*Ehyeh Aser Ehyeh*), in Greek ἐγώ εἰμί (*Ego Eimi*) "I EXIST"— not a being among beings, but the sheer act of Being Itself, *Ipsum Esse* ("to be"); and, Who, in the fullness of time, revealed Himself in Christ Jesus (Gal 4:4).

"God alone *IS* . . . God is the fullness of Being and of every perfection, without origin and without end" (*CCC* #213). This God, who is One God, who is Truth itself, who is Love itself, revealed Himself in three Persons: "God the Father," "God the Son," and "God the Holy Spirit" (*CCC* #253–255). In the words of Saint Athanasius— this is the catholic faith:

> That we worship One God in Trinity and the Trinity in Unity; neither blending their Persons nor dividing their Essence. For the Person of the Father is a distinct Person, the Person of the Son is another, the Person of the Holy Spirit still another. But, the Divinity of the Father, Son, Holy Spirit is One, their Glory equal, their Majesty coeternal.
>
> What quality the Father has, the Son has, the Holy Spirit has. The Father is Uncreated, the Son is Uncreated, the Holy Spirit is Uncreated. The Father is Immeasurable, the Son is Immeasurable, the Holy Spirit is Immeasurable. The Father is Eternal, the Son is Eternal, the Holy Spirit is Eternal. And yet there are not three eternal beings; there is but One Eternal Being. So too there are not three uncreated or immeasurable beings; there is but One Uncreated and Immeasurable Being.
>
> Likewise, the Father is Almighty, the Son is Almighty, the Holy Spirit is Almighty. Yet there are

not three almighty beings; there is but One Almighty Being.

Thus the Father is God, the Son is God, the Holy Spirit is God. Yet there are not three gods; there is but One God. Thus the Father is Lord, the Son is Lord, the Holy Spirit is Lord. Yet there are not three lords; there is but One Lord.

Just as Christian truth compels us to confess each Person individually as both God and Lord; so catholic faith forbids us to say that there are three gods or three lords.

The Father was neither made nor created nor begotten from anyone. The Son was neither made nor created; He was begotten from the Father alone. The Holy Spirit was neither made nor created nor begotten; He proceeds from the Father and the Son. Accordingly, there is one Father, not three fathers; there is one Son, not three sons; there is one Holy Spirit, not three holy spirits.

Nothing in this Trinity is before or after, nothing is greater or smaller; in their totality, the three Persons are coeternal and coequal with each other. Therefore, in everything, as was said earlier, we must worship their Trinity in their Unity, and their Unity in their Trinity.

Anyone then who desires to be saved should think thus about the Trinity. But it is necessary for eternal salvation that one also believe in the Incarnation of our Lord Jesus Christ faithfully.

Now this is the true faith:

That we believe and confess that our Lord Jesus Christ, God's Son, is both God and Man, equally. He is God from the Essence of the Father, begotten before time; and He is Man from the Essence of His mother, born in time. Completely God, completely Man, with a rational soul and human flesh. Equal to the Father, as regards to Divinity; less than the Father as regards to His Humanity.

APPENDIX A

Although He is God and Man, yet He is not two, but one Christ. He is one, however, not by His Divinity being turned into flesh, but by taking His Humanity into His Divinity. He is one, certainly not by the blending of His Essence, but by the unity of His Person. For just as one human is both rational soul and flesh, so too the one Christ is both God and Man.

He suffered for our Salvation; He descended to hell; He arose on the third day from the dead; He ascended to heaven; He is seated at the Father's right hand; from there He will come to judge the living and the dead. At His coming, all of humanity will arise bodily and give an accounting of their own deeds. Those who have done good will enter eternal life, and those who have done evil will enter eternal fire.

This is the catholic faith: one cannot be saved without believing it firmly and faithfully.[206]

| Saint Athanasius |

2. JESUS CENTRED: My theological focal point is *always* Christ Jesus. He should always be the *centre* of our lives. For it is God the Father's will and pleasure, that at the Name of Jesus every knee will bend (those in heaven, all those on this earth, and even all those in hell), and every tongue will confess, to the glory of God the Father, that Jesus the Christ is Lord (Phil 2:10–11).

With this truth, a second point becomes self-evident. Life is not about *you* or *me*. Yes, this is hard to digest in a self-centred, self-determining, *me-me* society. However, in the light of Christ, this truth becomes blatantly evident (cf. Phil 3:8). We must stop looking at ourselves and turn our gaze to Christ Jesus. Understanding fundamentals is not about getting caught up in theologizing; it is about getting caught up in Christ Jesus—opening ourselves to Him unconditionally, and thus proclaiming with gusto that we belong to Him.

3. CATHOLIC: These books are catholic in the sense of universal, pertaining to the entire Christian church. With this in mind, however, it is grounded in Catholic theology and Catholic teaching, with recognition of *apostolic succession*, an unbroken continuity, congruency, and authority of the Church rooted in and through the apostles, primarily Saint Peter, until the Second Coming of Christ (cf. Mt 16:18–19, Eph 2:20, and Ti 1:5).

In other words, I write this for the entire Christian church. However, I write this with total recognition of the authority and succession of all 266 popes and, if God wills, their successors (*Note*[207]). Hence, I assume that you are familiar with Catholic terminology and language. Nevertheless, if you belong to any other Christian group or denomination, these studies are still extremely beneficial. For if you are a true follower of Christ, a member of the universal church, your calling to live a Jesus-centred life is equally mandatory.

4. Theology: I am categorizing the word *theology* in two different ways: (i) academic theology and (ii) biblical-based theology (*Note*[208]).

The first, academic theology (that is, formal *academic* study or training), is essential for the good of the Church. However, not all Christians are called to engage in this category of theology. Academic theology can be left to individuals called by God to embark on such study for the *good* of the Church.

Therefore, when I use the word *theology* (unless otherwise noted), I am not talking about academic theology. I am more concerned with a foundational, biblical-based theology, upon which *all* Christians are called to embark (*Note*[209]). Learning and living, a biblical-based theology is a fundamental calling for *all* Christians. Our fundamental beliefs—or in other words, what we believe and our foundational thought structure—effect and thus produce the reality we live. It has been said: "When we believe right, we live right!" Alternatively, stated: "Faulty beliefs produce a faulty life."

5. Biblical-based Theology: So, what's a biblical-based theology? A biblical-based theology is based on a *biblical* understanding of God, which has stood the test of time, and that has been repeatedly reiterated and reinforced by the Saints and Church councils alike (*Note*[210]). Simplicity and practicality are in this theology.

Appendix A

By focusing on a foundational, biblical-based theology, we will avoid getting caught up in theological gymnastics, or having an elementary spirituality. Not only do both take us away from the truth, but also they inevitably lead us to pick apart the Gospel message to fit our own personal way of thinking. This is problematic.

On the one hand, we have been blessed with access to multiple theological resources that were not there a mere century ago. The Internet has also given us access to a plethora of theological information, unheard of even a decade ago. On the other hand, we are cursed by being bombarded with so much information that it sometimes becomes difficult for us to decipher the wheat from the chaff. There is so much craziness out there, so many interpretations, and so much misinformation that it can sometimes make our head spin to the point of giving up. With all these interpretations, we have now also divided Jesus into over thirty thousand[211] different denominations within the Christian family.

There will always be misuses of the Bible—it is a given. Remember that even Satan quotes the Bible to his advantage. He "masquerades as an angel of light" (2 Cor 11:14). He takes the sacred and profanes it, using it for evil ends. Therefore, it is vital for us to *know* what the Bible *actually* says, so we may protect ourselves against those who misrepresent and misinterpret it. Yes, we need to study the Bible to defend ourselves from those who will continually abuse it.

So, in one sense, the onus is on us to *really* know our faith. "Do not be carried away by all kinds of strange teaching" (Heb 13:9a). Do not trust every teaching, but test every teaching, and retain what is good (cf. 1 Jn 4:1 and 1 Thes 5:21). We must "beware of false prophets, who come to us in sheep's clothing, but underneath are ravenous wolves" (Mt 7:15). We must "be sober, vigilant, and alert; remember, that our opponent the devil is prowling around like a roaring lion looking for someone to devour" (1 Pt 5:8).[212] We must "resist him, steadfast and solid in our faith" (1 Pt 5:9).

To have a solid faith, we must be grounded in Sacred Scripture—a robust biblical-based theology—so nobody can sway us with falsehoods, with theological gymnastics, with feel-good spirituality, and with subjective personal prophecies or interpretations. "I say this so that no one may deceive you by specious arguments" (Col 2:4). "See to it that no one captivate you with an empty, seductive philosophy according to human tradition, according to the elemental powers of the world and not according to Christ" (Col 2:8).

Therefore, let us read our Bible cover to cover so we may be "steadfast and solid in our faith" (1 Pt 5:9). I cannot emphasize this enough. I am adamant on having a foundational, biblical-based theology, in which the interpretation is congruent with that of the Gospel message that was preached by the apostles.

"I am astonished on how we are so quick to forsake the One who called us, through the grace of Christ, for a different gospel (not that there is another)" (Gal 1:6–7).[213] We are so easily moved and convinced by "some out there who are disturbing and confusing us, and wish to pervert the Gospel of Christ" (Gal 1:7),[214] with a complicated theology, with a false feel-good spirituality, and subjective personal interpretations.

Even if the greatest orator, Internet sensation, television evangelist, self-proclaimed prophet, preacher, pastor, priest, "or even an angel from heaven should preach a gospel other than the one that the [apostles] have preached to us, let that one be accursed! Again, if anyone preaches to you a gospel other than the one that you received, let that one be accursed!" (Gal 1:8–9). We are not called to "currying favour with human beings" or to "seek to please people"—we are called to "be a slave of Christ" (Gal 1:10).

6. The Bible—Our Primary Source: "Ignorance of the Scriptures is ignorance of Christ" Saint Jerome asserts (*CCC* #133). Therefore, there is no way we can say we know Him if we do not know the Sacred Scriptures He has given us.

We need to know the Bible to understand Christ. How do we build and grow our Christian life when we have laid our foundation on sand? Won't it crumble? Won't it wash away? As Christ has taught us, we must build our foundation on a rock (Lk 6:48), on a solid foundation that can withstand any force (Lk 6:49).

Keeping with the analogy of a foundation, like a mason who mixes his mortar, we must also use the proper mix to build on a strong foundation. To do this, we must always start from the Bible, for

Appendix A

all Scripture is inspired by God and is useful for teaching, for refutation, for correction, and for training in righteousness, so that one who belongs to God may be competent, equipped for every good work. (2 Tm 3:16–17)

As a result, the Bible (Sacred Scripture) is *the primary source* of our Christian learning. As mentioned, I encourage all Christians to read the Bible cover to cover. I think by now I have pretty much heard all the excuses on why we do not read our Bible. Excuses notwithstanding, all it takes is a commitment.

For example, if you want to make a one-year commitment, read five chapters a day, five days a week, take the weekends off, and you will have completed the entire Bible (Old and New Testaments), in about one year. If five chapters a day is too much, read four, three, two, or even one. The key is to set an attainable goal for yourself (that will allow for prayerful reflection, absorption, integration, and application) and then go and accomplish it.

If you dislike reading, the Bible is available on audio CD or MP3. If you find listening too distracting, it is also available on DVD, where you can follow along with the words. That is to say, we have absolutely no excuses—all we need is to make that commitment, find a format that works for us, and just read it!

However keep in mind; we must *"Read the Scripture within 'the living Tradition of the whole Church'"* (CCC #113) (*Note*[215]). Therefore,

> Scripture must be read and interpreted with its Divine authorship in mind, no less attention must be devoted to the content and unity of the whole of Scripture, taking into account the Tradition of the entire Church and the analogy of faith.[216]
>
> | *Dei Verbum* |

To assist us in this task, we have two *secondary sources* that can help us interpret the primary source (the Bible). The first is the *Catechism of the Catholic Church* (promulgated by Saint John Paul II), which we are blessed to have, for it is a powerful tool that helps us understand the primary source and not misinterpret it. I am also an advocate of reading the *Catechism of the Catholic Church* cover to cover and having it as a reference and resource book in every Christian household. For the principal understanding, which undergirded the promulgation of the *Catechism of the Catholic Church*,

> was to guard and present better the precious deposit of Christian doctrine in order to make it more accessible to the Christian faithful and to all people of good will . . . [And] above all to strive calmly to show the strength and beauty of the doctrine of the faith.[217]
>
> | Saint John Paul II |

The second interpretation key and the final ingredient in the mix is the additional teachings handed down to us from those in authority: the Church councils, popes, and Saints, i.e., Sacred Tradition (*Note*[218]). Again, we are blessed that the Church, in Her wisdom, has preserved the teachings of the apostles and, in her authority, has handed down these teachings to us during the past two thousand years to keep us from going astray.

In brief, the primary source is the Bible (Sacred Scripture), and the two secondary sources are the *Catechism of the Catholic Church* and Church teachings. Mix this all together, and we have a solid foundation that will make us strong biblical-based theologians.

7. The Bible—Original Languages: The majority of the text, in what we refer to as the Old Testament, was originally written in the Hebrew language, some was written in Aramaic, and some in Greek.

It is also good to know that a few centuries before Christ the entire Old Testament Scriptures were translated into Greek. This translation is now referred to as the Septuagint, or the LXX, in reference to the tradition that seventy rabbis translated the text (*Note*[219]). Interestingly, the apostles (e.g., Saint Peter and Saint Paul), used not the Hebrew text, but this Greek text of the Old Testament Scriptures within the early church as they moved their preaching out of the Temple (and synagogues), and as they moved their

Appendix A

evangelization out of Jerusalem. Also, it is good to note that the New Testament writers used the Septuagint text a majority of the time when quoting Old Testament Scriptures within the New Testament.

Now, unlike the Old Testament, the New Testament was entirely written in Greek as the original language (*Note*[220]).

Why's this important to know? First, it is necessary, for when we say "the Word of God," we are referring to the original language; or to be precise, the underlying autograph text, and not any translation. Second, we must always have recourse to the original text among the many translations.

Stating these facts does not necessarily mean we need to learn biblical Hebrew or Greek to study the Word of God—even though that would be extremely beneficial (*Note*[221]). However, acknowledging and recognizing the original languages benefits our study of Scripture by adding nuance (and a deeper understanding) to a word or text, which a translation (English or otherwise) cannot accomplish. Therefore, from time to time I will use the original language to help us grasp this deeper understanding or subtle nuance within the underlying original text.

To give an example of the format I will use, let me use a word found in the Preface: ἀπολογία (apologia/*ap-ol-og-ee'-ah*). First, you will find the word in its original language, in this case, Greek. Then within the parentheses, you will find the phonetic spellings, a slash, followed by the pronunciation. If I use this word again, I reverse the order—e.g., *apologia* (ἀπολογία)—using the phonetically spelt word in *italics* and within parentheses the word in its original language I will, however, not repeat the pronunciation.

8. WORDS: We should not only be cautious in the words we use (for our words can be taken out of context), but we should also concern ourselves with the original meaning of the written word in its context, for context determines meaning.

Inherently, we recognize that most words have multiple or ambiguous meanings, categorized as either connotative (the secondary meaning or how a word is perceived) or denotative (the dictionary definition), and that words are equivocal (allowing the possibility of several meanings) more than univocal (having only one meaning). We also recognize that over time, some words even change in meaning.

As Christians, understanding that the same word can be used in multiple ways, and also that there is an evolution of words, is vital—for the meaning placed on a word is far more important than the actual *word* being used.

First, let us look at a *word* being used in multiple ways. The main problem we face in Scripture is when a word is used in a good sense or a bad sense. Interestingly, Saint Augustine addresses this issue back in his time.[222] Here are some examples. The word "tradition" is used in a good sense, "hold fast to the traditions, just as I handed them on to you" (1 Cor 11:2; also cf. 2 Thes 2:15), and in a bad sense, "see to it that no one captivate you with an empty, seductive philosophy according to human tradition" (Col 2:8; also cf. Mk 7:13). The word "wisdom" is used in a good sense, "the wisdom from above is first of all pure, then peaceable, gentle, compliant, full of mercy and good fruits, without inconstancy or insincerity" (Jms 3:17; also cf. Eph 1:17), and also in a bad sense, "wisdom of this kind does not come down from above but is earthly, unspiritual, demonic" (Jms 3:16; also cf. 1 Cor 1:12). Another word is "serpent." It is used in a good sense, "be wise as serpents" (Mt 10:16), and in a bad sense, "the serpent deceived Eve by his cunning" (2 Cor 11:3). The word "world" is also used in a good sense, "God so loved the world that He gave His only Son" (Jn 3:16), and in a bad sense, "Adulterers! Do you not know that to be a lover of the world means enmity with God?" (Jms 4:4). Even "bread" and "leaven" are used in a good sense, "I am the living bread that came down from heaven" (Jn 6:51), and "The kingdom of heaven is like yeast that a woman took and mixed with three measures of wheat flour until the whole batch was leavened" (Mt 13:33), and in a bad sense, "bread gotten secretly is pleasing" (Prov 9:17), and "Beware of the leaven of the Pharisees and Sadducees" (Mt 16:11). I hope you get the idea.

Second, we shall look at the evolution of words—the changing of the meaning of a word over time. The problem we as Christians face here is that some words have lost their objective meaning, and now have only a meaning determined by the user, (according to societal norms), which unfortunately most Christians have adopted. This issue has become a problem, for we have lost the true Christian

Appendix A

meaning of some words. Therefore, I will define words by their original biblical meaning in context. If I may paraphrase Saint Basil the Great:

> We must count terms used in theology and theological details as of primary importance. We must endeavour to trace out the hidden meaning of every word, every phrase, and every little syllable. This is a characteristic lacking in those who are idle in the pursuit of truth. But a distinguishing mark of those who pursue towards the goal, "the prize of God's upward calling, in Christ Jesus" (Phil 3:14). For the prize that is set before us—so far as is possible with human nature—is to be made like unto Him. Now without knowledge there can be no making like; and knowledge is not attained without lessons and study. The beginning of teaching is speech, and syllables and words are parts of speech. It follows then that to investigate syllables and words is not to shoot wide of the mark. Truth is always a quarry hard to hunt, and therefore we must look everywhere for its tracks. The acquisition of truth is just like that of other disciplines, crafts, or trades; it grows bit by bit—apprentices must despise nothing. If we despise the first elements as small and insignificant, we will never reach the perfection of wisdom.[223]

| Saint Basil the Great |

9. PRACTICAL APPLICATION: Theological study (i.e., a strong biblical-based theology) should be practical in and of itself. If not, we are merely embarking upon an academic exercise. One of the primary goals of this study is not only to help understand *Christian charity*, but also it is about helping us move from mere knowledge or theories into *practical application*. But to do this, we need accurate knowledge. We must make every effort to supplement our faith with knowledge (cf. 2 Pt 1:5). Yes, we strengthen our faith with the theological study, or theory.

Theories are necessary. They contain the foundational theological principles of Christianity that we stand on. Once we have these principles as our bedrock, we, however, cannot remain there—we must allow the movement from one to the other. We must move forward and apply these principles in our day-to-day *practical Christian living*—with the desire to live virtuous lives.

Our goal is *orthopraxy*.[224] That is to practise orthodox theology. So we have congruency between what we believe and how we live. This is what the Saints precisely have done. They demonstrate a holy *lived theology*.

As said, theological study (done properly) *is* the most practical study that we will ever embark upon, for it penetrates every facet of our lives and teaches us truths that no other study can do.

10. Analogy: When speaking about the Infinite, finite language always falls short. However, analogies, my own or borrowed, convey truths, or at the least help us better understand it. Analogies may also fall apart at one point. So, if they help, excellent. Use them. If they do not help, drop them and move on.

11. Paradox: A paradox, by the definition that Christians most commonly associate with the instances found in the Bible, is a statement or proposition that seems self-contradictory or absurd but in reality, expresses truth. For example, consider the statement, "Blessed are you who are poor" (Lk 6:20). At first glance, this statement seems absurd; but in reality, it conveys a profound truth—most of us are familiar with this example of a paradox, expressed in a single statement. However, less commonly recognized as a paradox are statements in the Bible that do not appear in the text, at the same place, but when placed side-by-side they *seem* contradictory (*Note*[225]).

For example, in the Gospel of Saint Matthew, we are told not to blow our trumpets (Mt 6:2), to give in silence and in secret (Mt 6:4) not letting our "left hand know what our right is doing" (Mt 6:3). However, in the chapter previous, we are told to be a light to the world (Mt 5:14), that we should "shine before others" (Mt 5:16), and not hide "under a bushel basket" (Mt 5:15), so others may *see* our "good deeds" and glorify God (Mt 5:16). At first glance, the commands may sound contradictory. Did Saint Matthew forget what

Appendix A

he wrote? How are we to do both without contradiction? However, again on closer examination, in proper contexts, we find that these two seemingly contradictory statements, in reality, also convey different, but equally valid truths.

However, here is the problem with these types of paradoxes. Because these are two completely separate statements, it is somewhat easy for us to be uninformed, to ignore, or reject, or to favour one statement that fits our way of thinking. In so doing, we inevitably move away from the full truth. This favouring is one reason why two people can use the same Bible, and with selective proof-texting, use only one of the statements out of context, to justify their respective position.

Similarly, this also applies to separate statements, one of which is capable of being interpreted as right-leaning and the other statement capable of being interpreted as left-leaning. This paradox also tends to pull us to one side or the other. I think it was Saint Augustine who said, "Holiness lies in the middle" (*Note*[226]). Yes, holiness and truth lie in holding both statements simultaneously and without contradiction or mitigation—recognizing the tension between the two.

On this note—although our personality may pull us toward one side or the other—as Christians, we should *not* be left-leaning or right-leaning, liberal or conservative. A Christian should be orthodox.[227] To paraphrase Saint Augustine: If we only believe what we like in Sacred Scripture, and reject what we do not like, it is not the Truth we believe, but ourselves. In view of that, whenever encountering these examples of paradoxical statements, we must hold both accounts without contradiction. Again, holiness and virtue often lie in the middle. Authentic Christianity is rarely either/or—it is usually both/and. As you might have heard, "Christian commitment is total and not selective."

12. Orthodox: Yes, we must strive for orthodoxy! This study is not a *soft* theology, meaning, this book is not a *feel-good* theology or spirituality. If you are looking for a theological take that is in line with the cultural tendency of exculpation, which says, "You're okay," "I'm okay," "We are all okay," you will be disappointed. If you are also looking for a left-leaning *liberal extremist* position or a right-leaning *conservative fundamentalist* position, you will be disappointed.

While we are on the subject, orthodoxy is not about being a moderate; do not confuse this with either *balance* or *moderation*, as proposed within secular thought, or unorthodox Christian thought. It is neither. It is about recognizing both truths (as stated above) and holding both realities simultaneously, without contradiction and without mitigation—an adherence to *Truth* in totality.

Appendix A

Endnotes

Preface

1. **Note:** "Today, many Christians are no longer even aware of the basic teachings of the Faith, so there is a growing danger of missing the path to eternal life" (Cardinal Gerhard Müller, *Manifesto of Faith*, February 8, 2019).

2. For further insight, refer to Timothy George, *Theology of the Reformers* (Nashville, Tennessee: Broadman & Holman Publishing Group), 195. According to Saint Augustine, another phenomenon occurs in the *very work of distribution* of God's work. Here is how he puts it: "The Lord saith 'Whosoever hath, to him shall be given' [Mt 25:29]. He will give, then, to those who have; that is to say, if they use freely and cheerfully what they have received, He will add to and perfect His gifts. The loaves in the miracle were only five and seven in number before the disciples began to divide them among the hungry people. But when once they began to distribute them, though the wants of so many thousands were satisfied, they filled baskets with the fragments that were left [Mt 14:20]. Now, just as that bread increased in the very act of breaking it, so those thoughts which the Lord has already vouchsafed to me with a view to undertaking this work will, as soon as I begin to impart them to others, be multiplied by His grace, so that, in this very work of distribution in which I have engaged, so far from incurring loss and poverty, I shall be made to rejoice in a marvellous increase" (Saint Augustine, *On Christian Doctrine*, book 1, chapter 1, number 1).

3. Author's translation.

Introduction

4. **Images:** See cover: "*Christ Crucified*" by Diego Velázquez, 1632; "*Jesus Washing Peter's Feet*" by Ford Madox Brown, c1852; "*The Good Samaritan*" by Dan Burr.

Chapter 1 | Charity: The Christian Perspective

5. **Theological Virtues:** "Faith, hope, and charity are the three theological virtues. Faith is a divinely infused virtue, which enables us to assent with conviction to the truths of salvation revealed by God. Hope is the infused virtue that enables us to rely on God's grace and salvation to look forward to achieving eternal salvation and fulfillment in Him. Charity is the infused virtue which enables us to love God for His own sake and oneself and others for His sake as well" (*Catholic Encyclopedia*).

---

6. *Note*: During the forty-day liturgical season of Lent, we engage in a spiritual renewal by fasting, special prayer, and *almsgiving* in order to prepare for Easter. As we will discover, *alms* connects to charity, and charity expresses Christian love.

7. Pope Benedict XVI, Encyclical Letter, *Deus Caritas Est* (*God Is Love*), number 2.

8. Ibid.

9. *Note*: My analysis here of the Greek words for *love* is very elementary. I am also analyzing only the three different Greek words for love found in Bible. My primary goal here is to help us understand the various nuances within the three different Greek words for love, in order to give us a richer understanding of the Scriptural text. For further insight, I would highly recommend that you read Anders Nygren, *Agape and Eros* (New York and Evanston: Harper & Row Publishers, 1969), or C. S. Lewis, *The Four Loves* (New York: Harcourt Brace, 1960).

10. *Note*: All three words, *agape* (ἀγάπη), *eros* (ἔρως), and *philia* (φιλία) are found in the Greek Old Testament, the Septuagint (also known as LXX; see *Appendix A*: (7) *The Bible: Original Languages*). In the Greek New Testament, only two of these words, *agape* (ἀγάπη) and *philia* (φιλία), are found.

11. *Note*: Contrary to some beliefs—and some Eastern thought (religious and philosophical)—love *cannot* be separated from suffering. If fact, we must learn that *true* love is connected to suffering. All we need to do is look at the Cross.

12. Pope Benedict XVI, Encyclical Letter, *Deus Caritas Est* (*God Is Love*), number 3.

13. Ibid.

14. *Note*: Even though this is a downward movement, we should not confuse this with *cupiditās*, which is more appropriately acquainted with "vulgar" *eros* (ἔρως).

15. See *Appendix A*: (7) *The Bible: Original Languages*.

16. Pope Benedict XVI, Encyclical Letter, *Deus Caritas Est* (*God Is Love*), number 3.

17. Ibid., number 5.

18. Ibid.

19. **Note**: This is *not* in the Platonic sense of a "heavenly *eros* (ἔρως)" — as in a yearning, a longing, or a desire to find something that is lacking within us, which we find in God. "The love of man for God which the New Testament speaks is of quite different stamp. It means a wholehearted surrender to God, whereby man becomes God's willing slave, content to be at His disposal, having entire trust and confidence in Him and desiring only that His will should be done" (Anders Nygren, *Agape and Eros*, New York and Evanston: Harper & Row Publishers, 1969, xvi-xvii).

20. Pope Benedict XVI, Encyclical Letter, *Deus Caritas Est* (*God Is Love*), number 3.

21. **Note**: "The God of [*agape* (ἀγάπη)] loves simply because it is His nature to love — and the children of God love because they take after their Father and delight to do as He does. [*Agape* (ἀγάπη)] is by nature so utterly self-forgetful and self-sacrificial that it may well seem (from egocentric point of view at any rate) to involve the supreme irrationality of the destruction of the self, as some critics have alleged that it does. But in fact, [*agape* (ἀγάπη)] means the death, not of itself, but of selfishness; it is the antithesis, not of selfhood, but of self-centredness, which is the deadliest enemy of true selfhood. Man realizes his true self just in so far as he lives by and in [*agape* (ἀγάπη)]. That is what he was created for by God, who is [*agape* (ἀγάπη)]" (Anders Nygren, *Agape and Eros*, New York and Evanston: Harper & Row Publishers, 1969, xxii).

22. **Note**: To be "open" and to "receive" are quite profound, for it is not only stated in a practical sense, it is also stated in a theological, and biological sense (cf. Eph 5:32). If this intrigues you so that you desire to know the theological (and biological) understanding that underlies this text, I would highly recommend that you go straight to the source and read Saint John Paul II's *Man and Woman He Created Them: A Theology of the Body* (Boston: Pauline Books & Media, 2006), and Karol Wojtyła (Pope John Paul II), *Love and Responsibility* (Boston: Pauline Books & Media, 2005). By the way, some might find these books are not easy reads; nevertheless, they are the foundational books on this topic.

23. **Note**: This is not in the sense of objectifying his wife, but in the sense of and outward movement or thrust, from husband to wife.

24. **Note**: There are only two places in the entire New Testament that a *charcoal fire* is mentioned; both are found in the Gospel of Saint John. Using the charcoal fire, Saint John subtly connects Peter's threefold denial of knowing Jesus (Jn 18:18ff.), with Peter's need of a threefold confession of love, to rehabilitate himself, so to speak, and to counteract his earlier threefold denial (Jn 21:9ff) which intriguingly, also occurs on "the third time Jesus was revealed to His disciples after being raised from the dead" (Jn 21:14).

25. *Note*: Looking at Jesus' encounters and dialogues with the Adulterous woman (Jn 8:3ff.), and the Samaritan woman (Jn 4:4ff.), we not only see His patience and respect for the person, we also see the invitation to a journey with Him and a call for interior conversion.

26. *Note*: Despite Pope Benedict XVI's comments in his Encyclical Letter, *Deus Caritas Est* (*God Is Love*), number 3, some scholars argue that *philia* (φιλία) is primary and *agape* (ἀγάπη) is secondary. Even though I agree with Pope Benedict XVI, and disagree with these scholars, I do not intend to enter into this argument. My goal is simply to state the *actual* word used in Sacred Scripture. As we have seen, Scripture itself uses *agape* (ἀγάπη) as the distinctive form of Christian love. Also keep in mind, if *philia* (φιλία) were primary, we would have a problem "loving" our enemy, would we not?

27. *Note*: It is important to note that all love is Christian love inasmuch as it participates and cooperates in and with God's love. Conversely, love is not Christian love, if it is separated from God's love.

Chapter 2 | Charity: It is an Act of the "Will"

28. Saint Thomas Aquinas, *Summa Theologica*, pt. I–II, question 59, article 4; also cf. Saint Thomas Aquinas, *Summa Theologica*, pt. I–II, question 26, article 4.

29. *Note*: "How was love misconstrued? Well, it is misconstrued as being a 'nice guy.' To be a person of love is to be a nice guy, a nice gal. Or, as Flannery O'Connor said, 'To have a heart of gold' . . . Or being a person of love is to be a 'gentleman.' Now again, nothing in the world is wrong with being a 'gentleman' or 'having a heart of gold' or being a 'nice guy,' but that isn't love. Love is 'willing the good of the other' and then doing something concrete about it. It is not an emotion; it is not an attitude; it is a move of the will to want the good of the other and do something about it. That's love. Now once you see that, you see that love is altogether reconcilable with not being a very nice guy, sometimes. Not being a gentleman, sometimes. You know what I mean is . . . 'tough-love.' If you are challenging someone who is caught in an addiction, you have to say some pretty tough things, some really strong demands, you're being anything but nice at that moment; but you are being a person of love. Or think of the call to conversion. The call to conversion is an ingredient in love. Why? Because love is wanting the good of the other. If someone is on the errant path, if someone is on a sinful state of life, the loving thing to do is to get them out of it, to shake them out of their complacency, to change them. So love is utterly reconcilable with being not a nice guy, being un gentleman-like. Love, as Dostoyevsky said, and Dorothy Day famously quoted him, 'is a harsh and dreadful thing.' Nice guys are not harsh and dreadful, but people of love can be because love is a willing of what is truly good for the other" (Bishop Robert Barron, "Faith, Hope, and Love," January 31, 2013, accessed September 5, 2016, 7:17, https://www.youtube.com/watch?v=PuyKsaj6GbM).

30. Pope Benedict XVI, Encyclical Letter, *Deus Caritas Est* (*God Is Love*), number 6.

31. Saint Thomas Aquinas, *Summa Theologica*, pt. II II, question 27, article 6; also cf. Saint Thomas Aquinas, *Summa Theologica*, pt. I II, question 27, article 1.

32. *Note*: This understanding is also stated by Saint Augustine, for "not any and every '*bonum*' can satisfy man's needs. As created by God, temporal things are good, but when He created them He never intended them to be objects of the man's love and desire in which man should seek his 'sufficiency' . . . Real rest and satisfaction can only be found in *the Highest Good* [*Summum Bonum*]; man cannot be content with anything less. If by pursuing some lower good he is prevented from seeking the Highest Good, then the lower good is no longer a good for him; it hinders him from attaining that which could satisfy him to a still higher degree" (Anders Nygren, *Agape and Eros*, New York and Evanston: Harper & Row Publishers, 1969, 490-491). Also here is a beautiful prayer from Saint Francis of Assisi: "All-powerful, most Holy, most High, Supreme God: all Good, Supreme Good, totally Good, You Who alone are Good, may we give You all praise, all glory, all thanks, all honor, all blessing, and all good. So be it! So be it! Amen" (Regis J. Armstrong O.F.M. Cap., ed., *Francis of Assisi: The Saint*, vol. I, *The Life of Saint Francis by Thomas of Celano*, New York: New City Press, 1999, 162).

33. Pope Benedict XVI, Encyclical Letter, *Deus Caritas Est* (*God Is Love*), number 17.

34. *Note*: "Many Catholics tend to think our goal is essentially to be good and make it to heaven. In fact, our goal is to extend the Kingdom of God on earth by making the world a place where Christ is known and loved, so that as many people as possible are brought with us to eternal life" (Archbishop Allen H. Vigneron, *Unleash The Gospel*, June 2, 2017).

35. *Note*: The opposite also hold true, for the worse act we can do is to take a person away from God (cf. Mt 18:6, Mk 9:42, and Lk 17:2).

36. Pope Benedict XVI, Encyclical Letter, *Deus Caritas Est* (*God Is Love*), number 6.

37. *Note*: Her is how Archbishop William E. Lori puts it (with some of my commentary in square brackets): "When we *truly* believe that God is love [remember *agape* (ἀγάπη): sacrificial, unconditional, self-giving love] (cf. 1 Jn 4:8) and that God loves us more than we could ever ask or imagine [an encounter that also engages our will and intellect], then we rediscover our calling to be men and women of true and *authentic charity* [Christian love: *agape* (ἀγάπη)] . . . Once we have fallen in love with God through faith [and our will aligns itself with His will], then we will want to share the truth of His

love and the love of His truth with those around, including family members and friends . . . The *greatest act of charity* we can offer others is to share with them the living Word of God [the *Summum Bonum*], to help them discover the gift of faith that opens them up to the love of God in their lives" (*emphasis* added) (Archbishop William E. Lori, *"Faith and Charity," Columbia*, February 2013, 4–5).

38. Saint Gregory the Great, *Catena Aurea*, Commentary on the Gospel of Saint John chapter 15.

39. *Note*: This understanding of love—to "will the good of the other" for the "sake of the other"—can be used as a tool or a check within our daily interactions with family and friends. In our daily interactions we can continually ask ourselves, am I "willing the good" of my father, my mother, my brother, my sister, my friend, my coworker, etc. In this particular action, discussion, or situation that I am having with them, am I truly willing their good, for their sake, and not mine. This is a practical and powerful test for us to use in our daily interactions.

40. *Note*: Here is the disposition that we must have. The image Scripture gives us is that we are *one body*. The finger is not envious of the arm, or the arm envious of the leg. The finger, the arm, and the leg work together in building the one body. Likewise, we should not be envious of any part of the one body. Our brother or sister's success is our success, and their loss is our loss. Let us not tear each other down; let us work in building each other—building the body of Christ!

41. *Note*: Some scholars argue that the unidirectional characteristic of *agape* (ἀγάπη) is problematic, for it undermines the reciprocal action of giving and receiving love, which in essence sustains and supports love. Yes, I agree that we cannot always give love we must also receive love. Now, this receiving of love may come from the source it is given to, as in the case of *eros* (ἔρως), and *philia* (φιλία), however, it does not necessarily have to come from the source it is given to, as in the case of *agape* (ἀγάπη). The practice of self-sacrificial, unselfish concern for the good of another, does not guarantee a reciprocal action. In fact, Christian *agape* (ἀγάπη) does not expect a reciprocal action (cf. Mt 5:46). That said, we as Christians do give what we receive, and that Source is God Himself—"We love because He first loved us" (1 Jn 4:19).

42. *Note*: At the end of this series of questions, Jesus tells us to "be perfect, just as [our] heavenly Father is perfect" (Mt 5:48). The English word *perfect* comes from the Greek word τέλειος (teleios/*tel'-i-os*), meaning to *complete* (in various applications of labor, growth, mental and moral character, etc.), or to bring to completion, or perfection; this word is rooted in the Greek word τέλος (telos/*tel'-os*), meaning the end result of an act or state, to *set out* for a definite point or *goal*, or an end propose. Therefore, based on the series of Jesus'

ENDNOTES

questions prior to this statement (and in the context of this study), to be *perfect*, means to complete the task of love, which is to love the just and the unjust (Mt 5:45), our neighbours and our enemies.

43. The Episcopal Commission for Doctrine of the Canadian Conference of Catholic Bishops, "Jesus and Salvation: A Lenten Reflection," 2014, 1.

44. C. S. Lewis, *The Complete C. S. Lewis Signature Classics: Mere Christianity* (New York, N.Y.: Harper One, 2007), 110.

45. Regis J. Armstrong O.F.M. Cap., ed., *Francis of Assisi: The Saint*, vol. I, *The Life of Saint Francis by Thomas of Celano* (New York: New City Press, 1999), 194.

46. *Note*: During a Lenten Mission, Bishop Emeritus Frederick Henry, suggested that in order to make 1 Corinthians 13:4 7 concrete and practical, we should read it by replacing the word "*love*" with our *own name*, and consequently make that a reality. Here is the text, try it (every time you see the word *love*, replace it with your own name): *love* is patient, *love* is kind, *love* is not jealous, *love* is not pompous, *love* is not inflated, *love* is not rude, *love* does not seek [his/her] own interests, *love* is not quick-tempered, *love* does not brood over injury, *love* does not rejoice over wrongdoing but rejoices with the truth; *love* bears all things, believes all things, hopes all things, endures all things (1 Cor 13:4 7). Now, go make that a reality!

Chapter 3 | Charity: It is Ethical and Moral

47. **Corporal Works of Mercy:** "Also defined as feeding the hungry, giving drink to the thirsty, clothing the naked, sheltering the homeless, visiting the sick, visiting the imprisoned and burying the dead. Of these, six are found in Matthew's account of the Judgment (Mt 25:34 40). The only one of this list not found in Matthew's Judgment scene is the last one burying the dead. Presumably, burying the dead was included in deference to the body's being the 'temple of the Holy Spirit' (1 Cor 3:16)" (*Catholic Encyclopedia*).

48. **Spiritual Works of Mercy:** "Also defined as instructing the ignorant, correcting sinners, advising the doubtful, showing patience to sinners and those in error, forgiving others, comforting the afflicted and praying for the living and dead" (*Catholic Encyclopedia*).

49. *Note*: Interestingly, it has been said that praying for the dead is the most unselfish form of love, for there is a guarantee of non-repayment.

50. Dorothy Day, *Catholic Quotations*, accessed September 5, 2016, https://catholicquotations.com/catholic-social-teaching/.

51. *Note*: A simple definition that I once heard is that *ethics* is how we treat the people we do not know—to build a society, a system.

52. *Note*: A simple definition that I once heard is that *morals* are how we treat the people we do know.

53. *Note*: I once heard; if our ethics that govern our society are ruled by subjective morals, which are projected on to others, we end up with a society that is governed by self-aggrandizement.

54. *The Liturgy of the Hours* (New York: Catholic Book Publishing Co., 1975), vol II, 969.

55. *Note*: Some have misunderstood the *principle of double effect* (also known as, the *doctrine of double effect*), by stating that it is permissible to do something harmful if it results in a greater good. This is not true. Although a harmful outcome might occur, the nature of the act must be good in and of itself (or at a minimum morally neutral). For example, the *CCC* states: "The legitimate defence of persons and societies is not an exception to the prohibition against the murder of the innocent that constitutes intentional killing. 'The act of self-defence can have a double effect: the preservation of one's own life; and the killing of the aggressor . . . The one is intended, the other is not'" (*CCC* #2263) (cf. *CCC* #1737 and Saint Thomas Aquinas, *Summa Theologica*, pt. II–II, question 64, article 7). It is also good to note the difference between formal and material cooperation. "Formal cooperation involves actually intending an evil purpose, regardless of the extent of physical participation in executing the act, e.g., advising, counseling, promoting, or condoning an evil act—all constitute formal cooperation. Material cooperation, on the other hand, is any type of cooperation in which one does not intend the evil effects, but only the good. When such material cooperation is immediate [direct], it amounts to the same as formal cooperation because it is a direct contribution to an evil act in which the cooperator shares the responsibility for the act. On the other hand, mediate [dependent on] material cooperation, which can be either proximate of remote, under certain conditions is sometimes justified and even necessary" (*Manual of Guidelines on Clinical-Ethical Issues* published by The Catholic Health Association, pg. 82–83).

56. *Note*: "The circumstances (and the consequences) of the act make up the third element of moral action. These are secondary to the evaluation of a moral act in that they contribute to increasing or decreasing the good-ness or badness of the act. In addition, the circumstances may affect one's personal moral responsibility for the act. All three aspects must be good—the objective act, the subjective intention, and the circumstances—in order to have a morally good act. This teaching, which recognizes both the objective and subjective dimension of morality, is often at odds with a perspective that views morality as a completely personal or merely subjective reality. In such a view, held by

ENDNOTES

some in our culture, there are no objective norms capable of demanding our moral compliance. Such a denial of an objective and unchanging moral order established by God results in a vision of morality and moral norms as being a matter of personal opinion or as established only through the consent of the individual members of society" (Bishop Emeritus Frederick Henry).

57. *Note*: It is of utmost importance that we as Christian gain an *informed conscience*! Thus, we must go and inform ourselves! To get started on this exploration, or to get some help to these or similar questions, please refer to the *CCC*. Almost every topic is indexed in the back.

CHAPTER 4 | CHARITY AND ITS ORDER

58. *Note*: I am using this term to mean the worldview of Philosophical Naturalism, also known as, Metaphysical Naturalism, and/or Secular Humanism, also known as Humanism. As a whole, this is the philosophical worldview that emphasizes the value of human beings, a progressive philosophy of life which affirms that the human person has the ability and responsibility to lead an ethical life of personal fulfillment that aspires to the greater good of humanity through the use of reason and ingenuity, without the need for theism and/or other supernatural and/or spiritual laws and/or beliefs.

59. *Note*: In addition, we should also note, Saint Paul and Saint James "each define faith differently. For James, faith is an intellectual assent to certain teachings, the type of mental activity even demons can perform (Jms 2:19). For Paul, however, faith is a personal commitment to Jesus the Christ as Saviour and Lord (Rom 10:9)" (William D. Mounce, ed., *Mounce's Complete Expository Dictionary of Old & New Testament Words*, Grand Rapids, Michigan: Zondervan, 2006, 594). Nevertheless for both, Saint Paul and Saint James, "faith" is only about knowing Christ Jesus — and nothing else — either by mind or by heart.

60. Mother Teresa, *A Call To Mercy* (New York: Crown Publishing Group, 2016), 276.

61. Pope Benedict XVI, Encyclical Letter, *Deus Caritas Est* (*God Is Love*), number 34.

62. *Note*: You might object to this. In actuality, a priest I know sternly objected. First, he stated, "I am in the world and I do what I do with the humanity that was given to me." Secondly, he went on to say, "I help people for their needs, out of a true concern for them, out of a true concern of who they are." These are valid objections. In actual fact, there is no ancient philosophy or modern social theory, no religion, or new age movement, which holds humanity in a higher regard than Christianity. However, as Christians, "we are in the world, but not of the world" (cf. Jn 17:16), therefore, we must always be rooted in

Christ, and what we do must always begin with Christ, if not it will be insufficient (cf. Saint Thomas Aquinas, *Summa Theologica*, pt. II–II, question 26, article 1).

63. *Note*: the impetus = Christ = the Why = the primary cause, which is to love Christ or for the love of Christ—versus—what we do = the secondary cause.

64. Jean-Baptiste Chautard, O.C.S.O., *The Soul of the Apostolate* (Charlotte, North Carolina: TAN Books, 1946), 90.

65. *Note*: It is only from the contemplative dimension (i.e., as Mary), that we are able to move into the apostolic dimension (i.e., as Martha), and avoid messing up the proper order to charity.

66. Thomas A Kempis, *The Imitation of Christ*, A Saint Joseph Giant Type Edition (New York: Catholic Book Publishing Co., 1969), book 1, chapter 15, number 3.

67. Anders Nygren, *Agape and Eros* (New York and Evanston: Harper & Row Publishers, 1969), 259-260.

68. *Note*: "The Catholic Church rejects nothing of what is true and holy in these religions . . . Yet She proclaims and is in duty bound to proclaim without fail, Christ who is the Way, the Truth and the Life (Jn 1:6)" (Vatican II, *Nostra Aetate: Declaration On The Relation Of The Church To Non-Christian Religions*, number 2).

69. *Note*: On a side note, some scholars argue that we cannot *agape* (ἀγάπη) God, for *agape* (ἀγάπη) is of God. Even though I disagree with these scholars, I do not intend to enter into this argument. My goal is simply to state the actual word used in Sacred Scripture. And, what we find is that Scripture itself uses *agape* (ἀγάπη) in all the text concerning our love for God (cf. Mt 22:37, Mk 12:30, and Lk 10:27).

70. *Note*: It is important to note that Judeo-Christian thought presupposes love of self. This is not our societal extreme of selfish or narcissistic love or an egocentric twisted form of love. Nor is it the opposite extreme, which denigrates and disrespects the self, treating the self as a mere object. It is however a healthy love of self. Christianity asserts that the human person (body, soul and spirit), is good (Gen 1:31). We are created "in the divine image" (Gen 1:27), and our "body is a temple of the Holy Spirit" (1 Cor 6:19). Thus, according to Saint Augustine, it is in our very nature to love our self. Now, if we were to analyze the way we love our self, we realize that it is not a condescending "there-there" love nor is it the aforementioned mistreating of self, or denigration of self. In fact, a healthy love of self should challenge the self; it might take forms of "tough-love" towards the self, as it respects and

takes care of the self. This love of self wants to "will the good" of the self. It is a love of self that does not go against God's will for the self. For we cannot claim to will the good of the self if we do not will God Himself. To will the good is to love God, Who is the true meaning of life itself. Therefore in essence, it is impossible to love God without love of self. And, it is impossible to love our neighbour without love of self, who interestingly is now close to the self. In addition, this love of self is also inherent when we consider the ultimate goal of Christianity. For example, unlike some Eastern thought (religious and philosophical), in which the ultimate goal of the soul is total annihilation (the cessation of reincarnation, thus the cessation of self) the ultimate goal of the Christian is resurrection (the eternal existence of body and soul with our Lord, thus the eternal existence of self). For this reason, Christians must have a healthy love of self to desire eternal existence with their Creator and Redeemer   and thus equally will that good towards their neighbour.

71. **Note:** Again, it is important to note that all love is Christian love inasmuch as it participates and cooperates in and with God's love. Conversely, love is not Christian love, if it is separated from God's love.

72. *The Liturgy of the Hours* (New York: Catholic Book Publishing Co., 1975), vol IV, 319.

73. **Note:** Saint Augustine continues by stating: "If you are holding your peace, through love hold your peace; if you are crying out, through love cry out; if you are correcting, through love correct; if you spare someone, through love spare: let the root of love within, of this root can nothing spring up but what is good" (Saint Augustine, *Ten Homilies on the 1st Epistle of John*, Homily number 8).

74. **Note:** "If you look at the matter clearly, because no one ought to love even himself for his own sake, but for the sake of Him who is the true object of enjoyment. For a man is never in so good a state as when his whole life is a journey towards the unchangeable life, and his affections are entirely fixed upon that. If, however, he loves himself for his own sake, he does not look at himself in relation to God, but turns his mind in upon himself, and so is not occupied with anything that is unchangeable. And thus he does not enjoy himself at his best, because he is better when his mind is fully fixed upon, and his affections wrapped up in, the unchangeable good, than when he turns from that to enjoy even himself" (Saint Augustine, *On Christian Doctrine*, book 1, chapter 22, number 21).

75. **Note:** "Worldly wisdom thinks that love is a relationship between man and man. Christianity teaches that love is a relationship between: man-God-man, that is, that God is the middle term . . . For to love God is to love oneself in Truth; to help another human being to love God is to love another man; to be helped by another human being to love God is to be loved" (Søren Kierkegaard, *Works of Love*, New York, N.Y.: Harper Perennial, 1962, 112-113). A

Christian "must always behave in a way that is worthy of the gospel of Christ" (Phil 1:27).

76. Timothy Keller, *The Meaning of Marriage: Facing the Complexities of Commitment with the Wisdom of God* (New York: Dutton Adult, 2011).

77. *Random House Webster's Dictionary.*

78. **Note:** To be clear, there are two extremes that we should avoid. The first extreme is to think that there can be love (or for that matter mercy or grace) without Truth. This extreme is a mistake that most liberal Catholics tend to make, which leads to hypocrisy. To this, the opposing extreme, which is just as problematic, is to think that Truth can be conveyed without love (mercy or grace). This extreme is a mistake that most conservative Catholics tend to make, which leads to brutality. Both of these extremes need to be avoided. Let us not separate Truth from love or love from Truth!

79. **Note:** This is a cautionary note and an admonition to all the shepherds reading this book (i.e., all the baptized who have been called to live and exercise the kingly and shepherdly roll of Christ Jesus). First, the cautionary note: we live in a society in which some words have become politically charged. Please get to know those words, and be very careful when you use them. Do not take it for granted that your sheep will understand how you are using those words (most likely, they will be taken within a secular context or narrative). If your statement (or word) is not clear, and thus is up for interpretation, you are doing an injustice to your sheep! Please spend time understanding the secular narrative, but be careful not to submit to it or sound like you are condoning it! Now to the admonition: shepherds, it is time to stop the nonsense! Your sheep are tired. There is too much disturbance within the shepherds. The *liberal* and *conservative* divide is tearing up our Church. When we look to our shepherds, we mainly see one of two types: the shepherd who pushes Truth without love; or, the shepherd who speaks of love without Truth. Rarely do we see a shepherd who is not afraid to speak the Truth in love! Again: "Love without truth is sentimentality; it supports and affirms us but keeps us in denial about our flaws. Truth without love is harshness; it gives us information but in such a way that we cannot really hear it" (Timothy Keller, *The Meaning of Marriage*). Shepherds remember that sheep are inherently stupid; therefore, we need you to teach us the Truth, *without ambiguity*, in love. Do not worry about being politically correct, or about currying favour (Gal 1:10). Do not be worried about alienating people because you speak the Truth (Jn 6:66) in love. Follow the example of the Good Shepherd and speak the Truth in love. For example: Then Jesus said, "Neither do I condemn you. Go, and from now on do not sin any more" (Jn 8:11; also cf. Jn 5:14). Do not pick one ("Neither do I condemn you") over the other ("Go, and from now on do not sin any more") or vice-versa. For if you speak both, the Truth in love and love in Truth, you have done your job properly as a good and faithful servant (Mt 25:21). However, if you

pick love over Truth or Truth over love, and lead your sheep astray, be prepared for the consequences (Mal 2:8 9, Mt 18:6, and 12:36 37), for you know that you will be judged by a higher standard and with a stricter condemnation (Jms 3:1 and Wisdom 6:6 8). Remember, shepherds, this is not a numbers game, or a popularity contest. Jesus does not change His message into what the listeners wanted to hear in order to bring them back (cf. Jn 6:60 64). No, He preached the Truth in love, whether they liked it or not. The rejection or acceptance of the message is up to those who listen (cf. Jn 6:67) please speak the *Truth in love*!

80. Pope Benedict XVI, Encyclical Letter, *Caritas in Veritate* (*Charity In Truth*), number 1.

81. *Note*: For an inspirational, practical application demonstrating the lived experience of the order to charity, I highly recommend the following book, especially the stories on page 89, and 91 92: *A Call To Mercy* (New York: Crown Publishing Group, 2016).

82. Mother Teresa, *The Face of God*, Lighthouse Catholic Media Audio CD.

Chapter 5 | Charity and the Law

83. *Note*: Some have also divided the law into three categories: (i) moral laws; (ii) ceremonial laws; and (iii) judicial laws.

84. William D. Mounce, ed., *Mounce's Complete Expository Dictionary of Old & New Testament Words* (Grand Rapids, Michigan: Zondervan, 2006), 392 393.

85. *Note*: "The Mosaic legislation has been superseded by God's action in Jesus Christ. Others understand end here in the sense that Christ is the goal of the law, i.e., the true meaning of the Mosaic law, which cannot be correctly understood apart from Him. Still others believe that both meanings are intended" (*NAB* footnote).

86. *Eschatology*: "The study and doctrines concerning the 'end times.' The English term is derived from the Greek adjective *eschatos* and refers to the 'teachings about the last things' (or 'end times'). The subject matter of the 'teachings' includes death, Christ's resurrection, the status of the dead prior to Christ's Second Coming (*parousia*), the general resurrection of the dead, heaven, hell, judgment, justice, etc." (*Catholic Encyclopedia*).

87. *Note*: "Tell me, you who want to be under the law, do you not listen to the law? For it is written that Abraham had two sons, one by the slave woman and the other by the freeborn woman. The son of the slave woman was born naturally, the son of the freeborn through a promise. Now this is an allegory. These women represent two covenants. One was from Mount Sinai, bearing children

for slavery; this is Hagar. Hagar represents Sinai, a mountain in Arabia; it corresponds to the present Jerusalem, for she is in slavery along with her children. But the Jerusalem above is freeborn, and she is our mother. For it is written: 'Rejoice, you barren one who bore no children; break forth and shout, you who were not in labor; for more numerous are the children of the deserted one than of her who has a husband.' Now you, brothers, like Isaac, are children of the promise. But just as then the child of the flesh persecuted the child of the spirit, it is the same now. But what does the scripture say? 'Drive out the slave woman and her son! For the son of the slave woman shall not share the inheritance with the son' of the freeborn. Therefore, brothers, we are children not of the slave woman but of the freeborn woman" (Gal 4:21-31).

88.   *Note*: Saint Augustine even takes it a step further by stating that if we rest "upon faith, hope, and love" (love being the greater), and if we keep a "firm hold upon these," we *do not* even need the Scriptures (Saint Augustine, *On Christian Doctrine*, book 1, chapter 39, number 43). Why is this so? It is because *everything* will cease (1 Cor 13:8), everything will pass away (1 Cor 13:9-10)—"everything" includes Scripture. So, what remains are faith, hope, and love (1 Cor 13:13a). But as we know, even among these three, faith will eventually yield to sight, and hope will eventually yield to possession, therefore what remains from these three is *love* (1 Cor 13:13b), as defined and understood in this study—"for *agape* (ἀγάπη) never fails" (1 Cor 13:8). In addition, to be clear, I am *not* saying this as stated by the Council of Trent: "If anyone shall say that nothing except faith is commanded in the Gospel, that other things are indifferent, neither commanded nor prohibited, but free, or that the ten commandments in no way pertain to Christians: let him be anathema [cf. n. 800]" (Pope Paul III, Council of Trent, *The Creed of the Catholic Faith is Accepted*, number 829, Can. 19). However, what I am saying is this as stated by the Council of Trent: "If anyone shall say that man can be justified before God by his own works which are done either by his own natural powers, or through the teaching of the Law, and without divine grace through Christ Jesus: let him be anathema [cf. n. 793 ff.]" (Pope Paul II, Council of Trent, *The Creed of the Catholic Faith is Accepted*, number 811, Can. 1).

89.   Søren Kierkegaard, *Works of Love* (New York, N.Y.: Harper Perennial, 1962), 118.

90.   Saint Augustine, *Ten Homilies on the 1st Epistle of John*, Homily number 8.

91.   *The Liturgy of the Hours* (New York: Catholic Book Publishing Co., 1975), vol VI, 1333.

92.   *Note*: Let me explain again using other vocabulary. You might have heard the terms the "spirit of the law," and the "letter of the law." Unfortunately, most use the term "spirit of the law" to the detriment of the "letter of the law" (as if they were somehow pitted against each other). To reduce the law to one or the

other is a grave mistake. For the spirit of the law never contradicts the letter of the law, and the letter of the law should be interpreted through the spirit of the law. Far from opposing each other, they are, in fact, in total harmony with each other. Now, let us connect these terms to the terms we have been using: the "letter of the law" we may call the commandments or the *law*, and, "the spirit of the law" we may call *agape* (ἀγάπη). We need both.

93. *Note*: "[Saint] Paul states that salvation comes through faith and not as a result of observing the Mosaic Law [Gal 5:13-18]. It is a free gift of God. A Christian is free, but [Saint] Paul qualifies Christian freedom. It is the freedom for love. One may ask: Do we need the ramifications of love and its application to life situations known as the laws? Yes, because of our limited human condition. If we were so mature in Christ that the compass of love would point out the direction unfalteringly, we could do without the laws that explain the ramifications of love in various human situations. Usually we are not. Laws are needed, but their observance should always be guided and motivated by love" (Rev. John C. Kersten S.V.D.).

94. *Note*: "The People of God is marked by characteristics that clearly distinguish it from all other religious, ethnic, political, or cultural groups found in history: . . . Its law is the new commandment to love as Christ loved us [cf. Jn 13:34]. This is the 'new' law of the Holy Spirit [cf. Rom 8:2 and Gal 5:25]" (*CCC* #782). "The Law of the Gospel fulfills the commandments of the Law. The Lord's Sermon on the Mount, far from abolishing or devaluing the moral prescriptions of the Old Law, releases their hidden potential and has new demands arise from them: it reveals their entire divine and human truth. It does not add new external precepts, but proceeds to reform the heart, the root of human acts, where man chooses between the pure and the impure [Mt 15:18 19], where faith, hope, and charity are formed and with them the other virtues" (*CCC* #1968). "The New Law is called a *law of love* because it makes us act out of the love infused by the Holy Spirit, rather than from fear; a *law of grace*, because it confers the strength of grace to act, by means of faith and the sacraments; a *law of freedom*, because it sets us free from the ritual and juridical observances of the Old Law, inclines us to act spontaneously by the prompting of charity" (*CCC* #1972).

95. *Note*: "The difference between the Judaic dispensation and the Christian is this, that in the former God demanded flight from sin and a fulfillment of the Law by the sinner, leaving him in his own weakness; but in the latter. God gives the sinner what He commands, by purifying him with His grace" (Pope Clement XI, Papal Bull, *Unigenitus: Condemnation of the Errors of Paschasius*, number 6).

96. *Note*: Do not think that the bar, so to speak, is raised arbitrarily, or raised without Jesus giving us the ability and infusing us with the grace to carry out the task. In Christ, we are able to carry out the law of love, and we are given

the ability to carry out the law of love, as long as we are open to His grace and we participate with His grace. In spite of our faults and failings, as followers of Christ we strive and move towards perfection in Christ Jesus. However, keep in mind that this movement is circular. "We love because He first loved us" (1 Jn 4:19). It is in His love that we are able to carry out the law of love, thus obeying His commandments (1 Jn 5:2). Rooted in the law of love is for us to "bear one another's burdens" (Gal 6:2), and to "serve one another through love" (Gal 5:13). In this we keep his commandments fulfilling the law of love—the law of Christ (Gal 6:2). And His commandments are not burdensome (1 Jn 5:3), for it is centred on Him, not on us!

97. Pope Benedict XVI, Encyclical Letter, *Deus Caritas Est* (*God Is Love*), number 1.

98. John Piper, *Desiring God: Meditations of a Christian Hedonist* (Colorado Springs, Colorado: Multnomah Books), 206.

99. *The Liturgy of the Hours* (New York: Catholic Book Publishing Co., 1975), vol III, 277.

Chapter 6 | Charity and the Good Samaritan Model

100. Dorothy Day, *Catholic Quotations*, accessed September 5, 2016, https://catholicquotations.com/catholic-social-teaching/.

101. *Note:* Donating via a reputable charitable organization has its place. Looking at Scripture, even Jesus healed the royal official son who was ill, without going to Capernaum (Jn 4:46–54). Therefore, if we have the ability to help others without going there, we should. Nevertheless, we must keep in mind, that this was the exception, not the rule.

102. *Note:* Let us not give to the poor for the sake of the poor; let us give to the poor for the sake of Christ Jesus. This must be our disposition; it is a disposition that most Christians do not get! In addition, within this disposition we find a deeper realization, namely, that in the true sense of the word we do not "give" to the poor. No, we "share" with the poor. Christ Jesus has blessed us; therefore we share what is His. Yes, we share with others what is His; it is nothing of our own!

103. Peter Kreeft, *Winning The Culture War*, Lighthouse Catholic Media Audio CD (*Note:* This is a paraphrase of the audio text).

104. *Note:* To be clear, this is not about *not* getting involved in causes for change; which if we are called to do we should.

Endnotes

105. *Note*: C. S. Lewis calls this thought pattern the "the subtlest of all snares." Stating it in different terms, here is what he says: "There have been men before now who got so interested in proving the existence of God that they came to care nothing for God Himself . . . There have been some who were so occupied in spreading Christianity they never gave a thought to Christ . . . Did ye never know a lover of books that with all his first editions and signed copies had lost the power to read them? Or an organizer of charities that had lost all love for the poor?" (C. S. Lewis, *The Complete C. S. Lewis Signature Classics: The Great Divorce*, New York, N.Y.: Harper One, 2007, 505 506).

106. *Note*: Keep in mind that we are most likely an "unspectacular idiot" to someone else! So, let us bear with one another with all humility, gentleness, patience, and through love (Eph 4:2; also cf. Col 3:13), for none of us are perfect!

107. Mother Teresa, *A Call To Mercy* (New York: Crown Publishing Group, 2016), 185.

108. Ibid., 174 175.

109. *The Beatitudes*: "Refers to the pronouncements (eight statements of Our Lord delineating the qualities of one who aspires to blessedness) found in Matthew 5:3 12 and Luke 6:20 23" (*Catholic Encyclopedia*).

110. *Note*: "God is to be loved for His own sake, and our neighbour for God's sake" (Saint Augustine, *On Christian Doctrine*, book 2, chapter 7, number 10). Or, in other words, "All others must be loved for Jesus' sake, but Jesus for Himself alone" (Thomas A Kempis, *The Imitation of Christ*, A Saint Joseph Giant Type Edition, New York: Catholic Book Publishing Co., 1969, book 2, chapter 8, number 2).

111. Note: The answer to the question "Who is my neighbour?" should not vary depending on our culture or society. The answer to this question comes from Jesus. Simply put, our neighbour is the one right next to us. The adage "loving local" has its merits.

112. Pope Benedict XVI, Encyclical Letter, *Deus Caritas Est* (*God Is Love*), number 34.

113. Pope Benedict XVI, Encyclical Letter, *Spe Salvi* (*Saved In Hope*), number 38.

114. *Note*: If we listen to His word, let Him live in us, and become doers of His word, we are "like a person building a house, who dug deeply and laid the foundation on rock; when the flood came, the river burst against that house but could not shake it because it had been well built. But the one who listens and does not act is like a person who built a house on the ground without a

foundation. When the river burst against it, it collapsed at once and was completely destroyed" (Lk 6:48–49; also cf. Mt 7:24–27). Yes, we must be "doers of the word and not hearers only, deluding ourselves. For if anyone is a hearer of the word and not a doer, he is like a man who looks at his own face in a mirror. He sees himself, then goes off and promptly forgets what he looked like. But the one who peers into the perfect law of freedom and perseveres, and is not a hearer who forgets but a doer who acts, such a one shall be blessed in what he does" (Jms 1:22–25).

115. *Enabling*: The word "enabling" can be used in a positive or a negative sense. In a positive sense, the term "enabling" is akin to empowerment (i.e., to provide means, to equip, to give power, competence, or ability to). In a negative sense, "enabling" is associated with the encouragement of dysfunctional behaviour (i.e., when a person directly or indirectly supports the self-destructive or addictive behaviour of another). Here, I am using the word "enabling" in the *negative* sense and the word "serving" to convey its positive meaning.

116. *Note*: A good example of this is found within Scripture. Saint Peter, following what we would today call political correctness or groupthink, acts in a manner contrary to the Gospel (Gal 2:11-14). Saint Paul sternly rebukes and opposes this act. This rebuking of Saint Peter by Saint Paul is totally congruent with *agape* (ἀγάπη); and may I also say, absolutely necessary. It is also important to note that we get a vast amount of teachings on *agape* (ἀγάπη) from Saint Paul, including the beautiful personification of love found in 1 Corinthians (1 Cor 13:1-13).

117. *Note*: "It is written: 'Give to the godly man, and help not a sinner' (Sirach 12:4). The latter clause of this sentence seems to forbid benevolence; for it says, 'help not a sinner.' Understand, therefore, that 'sinner' is put figuratively for sin, so that it is his sin you are not to help" (Saint Augustine, *On Christian Doctrine*, book 3, chapter 16, number 24).

118. *Note*: To be clear, this is society's articulation not mine. I am not advocating either unless it is grounded in Christ. For example, "the pursuit of happiness" can be fleeting. It is therefore better to pursue "meaningfulness" or "joyfulness."

119. *Prudence*: "A cardinal virtue along with justice, fortitude (courage) and temperance (moderation). Prudence enjoys a special place in the moral life because it has qualities of both intellectual and moral virtue. As an intellectual virtue, prudence guides the doer in choosing a way of accomplishing something (a means and a manner) which keeps the entire good in mind. Thus, prudence consults the demands of the other virtues in a situation of choice, making sure no aspect of the human good coming within the scope of the action is violated or neglected" (*Catholic Encyclopedia*).

120. ***Cardinal Virtues***: "Prudence, justice, temperance and fortitude are the cardinal virtues. They are the habits or powers developed by a person through practise, which are the source of, and controlling influence over, all other virtues. All other virtues are specifications or modifications of these four virtues, which are the standard of right reason and of all moral action" (*Catholic Encyclopedia*).

121. ***Note***: Jesus tells us: "The poor you will always have with you" (Mt 26:11, Mk 14:7, and Jn 12:8). Keeping this in mind, I would like to use what Jesus says about eunuchs (Mt 19:12), by applying this to the poor (mainly within western society). Granted what I am about to say may be controversial, nevertheless, *there are some who are poor because they were born so; some, because they were made so by others or society, and; some, because they have made a personal decision (this could be for the sake of the Kingdom), or more than likely for their own sake.* No matter what group they belong to, we are called to love them. For we are our "brother's keeper" (Gen 4:9).

122. ***Sloth***: Is one of the Capital Sins (a.k.a., Capital Vices or Deadly Sins). "The sin of sloth, involving a lack of enthusiasm for spiritual growth and development, is the antithesis of love of God and leads to undue love of pleasure, discouragement and ultimately despair" (*Catholic Encyclopedia*). This is the primary definition of "sloth." An overall *laziness* or idleness is only a secondary definition, which is how I am using it here.

123. ***Note***: Keep in mind, the ultimate *purpose* of life is rooted in Christ Jesus Himself!

124. ***Note***: There is also a relationship between rights and responsibility. It has been said that rights comes with responsibility; i.e., the purpose of rights is so we can dispense our responsibility.

125. ***Providence of God***: "Divine Providence is the plan by which God orders all things to their true end. While the plan itself is an act of divine wisdom, it presupposes the willing of an end or goal. Hence, in the first place, divine Providence is itself eternal, identical with the knowledge and will of God. Since God is the universal cause of all causes, nothing escapes His Providence. Moreover, divine Providence embraces the 'hidden plan' that God made 'in Christ as a plan for the fullness of time, to unite all things in Him, things in heaven and things on earth'" (Eph 1:9 10) (*Catholic Encyclopedia*).

126. ***Note***: We may argue that if we are truly detached we will not "feel the pain" which is an interesting argument.

127. ***Note***: There is a good article entitled *Time and Presence* by Archbishop William E. Lori (*Columbia*, December 2018, 4).

128. *Note*: We can also look at the poor widow in the Old Testament and her interaction with Elijah (see 1 Kgs 17:10–16). Interestingly, her story ends with a miracle.

129. *Note*: There are many facets to tithing. My goal here is to keep it very simple, concentrating and concerned with our personal disposition, more than the word "tithe" or even tithing itself.

130. *Note*: For a further study concerning first-fruits, see Saint Thomas Aquinas, *Summa Theologica*, pt. II–II, question 86, article 4. And, concerning tithing 10 percent, see Saint Thomas Aquinas, *Summa Theologica*, pt. II–II, question 87, article 1.

131. *Note*: Pope Leo XIII, in his encyclical *Rerum Novarum* (*On the Condition of the Working Class*, number 36) states, on the one hand: "No one, certainly, is obliged [even though we should as stated in Issues Number 4] to assist others out of what is required for his own necessary use or for that of his family," nevertheless, on the other hand, "when the demands of necessity [basic needs] and propriety [a decent appropriate life] have been met, it is a duty to give to the poor" (cf. Canon Law 222 §2). In actuality, we may argue that the remaining belongs to the poor!

132. *Note*: Just to be clear, there is a difference between donating via a charitable organization, and providing for our Church's needs (cf. *CCC* #2043), the latter of which we are *called* to do (2 Cor 9:5–8). It is also good to remember that there is a difference between giving out of an obligation or to fulfill a set requirement (i.e., the law), verses giving out of love.

133. *Note*: Concerning these organization, as Christians, we need to be aware of the cost (monetarily *and* otherwise), and is that *cost* justifiable (see Chapter 3, Charity: It is Ethical and Moral). Now, just an example from a monetary point of view, here are the top-incomes in some notable charities: World Vision, the top earner made $534,505; Boy Scouts of America, the top earner made $1,351,724*; Samaritan's Purse, the top earner made $713,846; Food for the Poor, the top earner made $470,120; Catholic Relief Services, the top earner made $468,999; Catholic Charities USA, the top earner made $503,140*; Boys & Girls Clubs of America, the top earner made $847,189 (and spent $124 Million just on fundraising); Habitat for Humanity International, the top earner made $372,969 (and spent $131 Million just on fundraising); United Way Worldwide, the top earner made $1,236,611 (and spent $310 Million just on fundraising)*; UNICEF (the U.S. arm), the top earner made $652,425; Make-A-Wish Foundation of America, top earner made $615,424; Feed the Children, top earner made $509,348; and, American Cancer Society, top earner made $2,569,668 (and spent $142 Million just on fundraising)—(Forbes, *The 100 Largest U.S. Charities*, Fiscal Year ending between June 30 and December 31, 2017, *December 31, 2015—all amounts are in U.S. dollars).

134. Pope Benedict XVI, Encyclical Letter, *Caritas in Veritate* (*Charity In Truth*), number 47.

135. Ibid.

136. Pope Benedict XVI, Encyclical Letter, *Spe Salvi* (*Saved In Hope*), number 35.

137. *Note:* By holding this paradox, we are kept from error. For some philosophers have argued that if there is nothing we can do through our works, this earthly life is pretty much insignificant or useless. Others argue that our life then is also fatalistically predetermined (because there is nothing we can do about it). By understanding this paradox, we realize that arguments and conclusions such as these do not hold.

138. *Note:* The assertion or phrase, *sola fide* — faith alone — is not found anywhere in New Testament writings, except once in the negative — "*not* by faith alone" (Jms 2:24; *emphasis* added). Luther, in order to give credence to his assertion, added the word *alone* (*allein* in German) to Romans 3:28. This word — alone or even only — is not in the original Greek text. Here is the German Luther Bible (GLB) translation of Romans 3:28: "So halten wir nun dafür, daß der Mensch gerecht werde ohne des Gesetzes Werke, *allein* durch den Glauben" (*emphasis* added). In addition, he wanted to remove the Epistle of Saint James from the Canon of Scripture. For in-depth exploration on *sola fide*, I would recommend reading *Not By Faith Alone*, by Robert A. Sungenis (Santa Barbara, CA: Queenship Publishing, 1997).

139. *Note:* "Against classical Lutheran doctrine, Catholic Faith holds that faith without good works is not sufficient to merit justification, for good works show one's willingness to cooperate with the initiatives of grace. Catholic doctrine rejects any notion that justification comes about through an 'inwardness' or merely a disposition, but it also objects to the mere performance of a physical act (*actus externus*) without an inward disposition of faith, hope, and charity. What is necessary for salvation is a faith that represents itself both externally through acts and internally through faith. That works are clearly required in the New Testament for union with Christ is seen in the many parables such as the Good Samaritan, Lazarus and Dives, and others. The true disciple of Jesus is one who labors in the vineyard, who tills the soil, who proclaims the Good News" (*Catholic Encyclopedia*).

140. *Note:* "'Man attains blessedness by a series of acts which are called merit,' writes Saint Thomas Aquinas. But, in saying this, he does not intend to diminish the significance of divine Grace or to transfer the stress in the matter of salvation from God to man himself. On the contrary, he most emphatically rejects the idea that men might acquire blessedness in his own strength" (Anders Nygren, *Agape and Eros*, New York and Evanston: Harper & Row Publishers, 1969, 621). "If anyone shall say that man can be justified before

God by his own works which are done either by his own natural powers, or through the teaching of the Law, and without divine grace through Christ Jesus: let him be anathema [cf. n. 793 ff.]" (Pope Paul II, Council of Trent, *The Creed of the Catholic Faith is Accepted*, number 811, Can. 1).

141. *Note*: this is the *Amplified Bible* translation; the input is not mine.

Chapter 7 | Charity and Mercy

142. Pope Benedict XVI, Regina Caeli message on Divine Mercy Sunday, March 30, 2008.

143. *Note*: In the Apostolic Exhortation, *Evangelii Gaudium* (*The Joy of the Gospel*), number 37; footnote number 39, cf. Saint Thomas Aquinas, *Summa Theologica*, pt. I–II, question 66, article 4–6. Saint Thomas explains that, "as far as external works are concerned, mercy is the greatest of all the virtues: 'In itself mercy is the greatest of the virtues, since all the others revolve around it and, more than this, it makes up for their deficiencies. This is particular to the superior virtue, and as such it is proper to God to have mercy, through which His omnipotence is manifested to the greatest degree'" (Pope Francis, Apostolic Exhortation, *Evangelii Gaudium*, *The Joy of the Gospel*, number 37; footnote number 41, cf. Saint Thomas Aquinas, *Summa Theologica*, pt. II–II, question 30, article 4). "We do not worship God with sacrifices and exterior gifts for Him, but rather for us and for our neighbour. He has no need of our sacrifices, but He does ask that these be offered by us as devotion and for the benefit of our neighbour. For Him, mercy, which overcomes the defects of our devotion and sacrifice, is the sacrifice which is most pleasing, because it is mercy which above all seeks the good of one's neighbour" (Saint Thomas Aquinas, *Summa Theologica*, pt. II–II, question 30, article 4). "Mercy is the externally visible and effectively active aspect of the essence of God, who is love (1 Jn 4:8; 16). Mercy expresses God's essence, which graciously attends to and devotes itself to the world and to humanity in ever new ways in history. In short, mercy expresses God's own goodness and love. It is God's *caritas operativa et effectiva*. Therefore, we must describe mercy as the fundamental attribute of God" (Cardinal Walter Kasper, *Mercy: The Essence of the Gospel and the Key to Christian Life*, New Jersey: Paulist Press, 2013, 88). And, to paraphrase Fr. Michael Schmitz: mercy is to put love into action; it is loving the unlovable; forgiving the unforgivable; it is the highest form of love; it is a particular mode of love (Fr. Michael Schmitz, *Could God Love Someone Like Me?*, Lighthouse Catholic Media Audio CD).

144. *Note*: I am using "human sin" in this statement; however, I will leave it up to the scholars to decide if it is human sin or the sin of the angels. For this study, that is neither here nor there. What is important, however, is the understanding that we are unable to say, "God is mercy," until after this point of sin (whichever sin it may be).

ENDNOTES

145. **Note**: In Gordon Clark's study of the predominate Hebrew word for mercy *hesed* (חֶסֶד), concludes that, "while [*hesed* (חֶסֶד)] is used with both God and humans as agent, the patient is always human but never Divine" (Gordon R. Clark, *The Word Hesed in the Hebrew Bible*, England: Sheffield Academic Press, 1993, 259).

146. Saint, Pope John Paul II, Encyclical Letter, *Dives In Misericordia* (On The Mercy of God), number 8.

147. Dr. Chad Pecknold (Associate Professor of Systematic Theology at the Catholic University of America,).

148. **Note**: This is how Bishop Robert Barron, puts it in one of his YouTube recordings: "The Church . . . is *extreme* in its demand, and it's *extreme* in its mercy. So, it holds up a very high objective moral ideal, *and* it has a very high sense of compassion and care for those who are struggling to integrate that high moral ideal. And, it's not a zero-sum game. That's the trouble . . . If you say mercy very strongly that means you have to dial-down the ideal, or if you dial-up the ideal, you had better dial-down the mercy. No, it's not a zero-sum game it doesn't work that way! The logic of Catholicism is a radical both-and-logic. We make an extreme demand and we express extreme mercy. That I think is the key!" (Bishop Robert Barron, June 2, 2016, accessed February 23, 2019, https://www.youtube.com/watch?v=-5ruTwxiLqs).

149. **Note**: For those of you who are interested, here is an abridged version of footnote number 52, from *Dives In Misericordia*: "In describing mercy, the books of the Old Testament use two expressions in particular, each having a different semantic nuance. First, there is the term *hesed*, which indicates a profound attitude of 'goodness.' When this is established between two individuals, they do not just wish each other well; they are also faithful to each other by virtue of an interior commitment, and therefore also by virtue of a faithfulness to themselves. Since *hesed* also means 'grace' or 'love,' this occurs precisely on the basis of this fidelity. The fact that the commitment in question has not only a moral character but also almost a juridical one makes no difference. When in the Old Testament the word *hesed* is used of the Lord, this always occurs in connection with the covenant that God established with Israel. This covenant was, on God's part, a gift, and a grace for Israel. Nevertheless, since, in harmony with the covenant entered into, God had made a commitment to respect it, *hesed* also acquired in a certain sense a legal content. The second word which in the terminology of the Old Testament serves to define mercy is *rahamim*. This has a different nuance from that of *hesed*. While *hesed* highlights the marks of fidelity to self and of 'responsibility for one's own love' (which are in a sense masculine characteristics), *rahamim*, in its very root, denotes the love of a mother (*rehem* = mother's womb). From the deep and original bond indeed the unity that links a mother to her child there springs a particular relationship to the child, a particular love. Of this love, one

Endnotes

can say that it is completely gratuitous, not merited, and that in this aspect it constitutes an interior necessity an exigency of the heart. It is, as it were, a 'feminine' variation of the masculine fidelity to self expressed by hesed. Against this psychological background, *rahamim* generates a whole range of feelings, including goodness and tenderness, patience and understanding, that is, readiness to forgive."

150. William D. Mounce, ed., *Mounce's Complete Expository Dictionary of Old & New Testament Words* (Grand Rapids, Michigan: Zondervan, 2006), 447.

151. Gordon R. Clark, *The Word Hesed in the Hebrew Bible* (England: Sheffield Academic Press, 1993), 267.

152. William D. Mounce, ed., *Mounce's Complete Expository Dictionary of Old & New Testament Words* (Grand Rapids, Michigan: Zondervan, 2006), 426.

153. *Note*: A simple definition that I once heard is that *grace* is we receiving all the good things (favour) that we do not deserve. Moreover, that through Jesus we receive all the good things (favour) that only He deserves.

154. *Note*: A simple definition that I once heard is that *mercy* is we not receiving all the bad things (or punishment) that we deserve. Moreover, that Jesus takes on or receives the bad things (or our punishment) that we should justly deserve.

155. *Note*: Interestingly, Saint Augustine had a broader and complex view of *cāritās* (charity). One may argue that it is almost a combination of the descriptions we have given here for both *agape* (ἀγάπη) and *eros* (ἔρως) (see Anders Nygren, *Agape and Eros*, New York and Evanston: Harper & Row Publishers, 1969, 476-484).

156. William D. Mounce, ed., *Mounce's Complete Expository Dictionary of Old & New Testament Words* (Grand Rapids, Michigan: Zondervan, 2006), 1040.

157. *Catholic Encyclopedia.*

158. *Note*: To be clear, the forgiveness that we give differs from Divine forgiveness. That said, as a Christian, we participate in Divine mercy (not in the sense that we offer salvation, or that our forgiveness can give salvation), we nevertheless lead others to Christ (i.e., Salvation) through the Church and Her Sacraments.

159. *Catholic Encyclopedia.*

160. *Note*: "But although Christ died for all [2 Cor. 5:15], yet not all receive the benefit of His death" (Pope Paul III, Council of Trent, *The Creed of the Catholic Faith is Accepted*, number 795).

161. *Note*: "[W]e may not downplay God's mercy and make God a fool, who, with liberal leniency, overlooks our mistakes and malice and lets them simply run wild in us" (Cardinal Walter Kasper, *Mercy: The Essence of the Gospel and the Key to Christian Life*, New Jersey: Paulist Press, 2013, 53).

162. *Note*: Do not allow anyone to lead you astray; mercy and forgiveness comes only with repentance. "John the Baptist appeared in the desert proclaiming a baptism of repentance for the forgiveness of sins" (Mk 1:4). Jesus begins His ministry by calling us to repentance — "Repent, and believe in the gospel" — He exclaims (Mk 1:15). "Thus it is written . . . that is repentance, for the forgiveness of sins, would be preached in His name to all the nations" (Lk 24-46-47).

163. *Note*: "I APPEAL to you therefore, brethren, *and* beg of you in view of [all] the mercies of God, to make a decisive dedication of your bodies [presenting all your members and faculties] as a living sacrifice, holy (devoted, consecrated) and well pleasing to God, which is your reasonable (rational, intelligent) service *and* spiritual worship" (Rom 12:1) (this is the *Amplified Bible* translation; the input is not mine).

164. *Note*: "Whoever blasphemes against the Holy Spirit never has forgiveness, but is guilty of an eternal sin" (Mk 3:29; also cf. Mt 12:32 and Lk 12:10.). "There are no limits to the mercy of God, but anyone who deliberately refuses to accept His mercy by repenting, rejects the forgiveness of his sins and the salvation offered by the Holy Spirit. Such hardness of heart can lead to final impenitence and eternal loss" (*CCC* #1864). "God predestines no one to go to hell; for this, a willful turning away from God (a mortal sin) is necessary, and persistence in it until the end. In the Eucharistic liturgy and in the daily prayers of Her faithful, the Church implores the mercy of God, who does not want 'any to perish, but all to come to repentance'" (2 Pt 3:9) (*CCC* #1037).

165. *Catholic Encyclopedia.*

166. *Note*: God's almighty power is in no way arbitrary: "In God, power, essence, will, intellect, wisdom, and justice are all identical. Nothing therefore can be in God's power which could not be in His just will or His wise intellect" (Saint Thomas Aquinas, *Summa Theologica*, pt. I, question 25, article 5) (*CCC* #271).

167. William D. Mounce, ed., *Mounce's Complete Expository Dictionary of Old & New Testament Words* (Grand Rapids, Michigan: Zondervan, 2006), 592-593.

168. *Note*: In moral theology, justice is giving to another what is justly due. "There are two standards for determining this: an arithmetical and a geometric standard. The arithmetical standard requires that the debtor give exactly the same amount to the other, while the geometrical standard requires only a proportional compensation for what was received. Commutative justice

ENDNOTES

regulates actions between individuals, while distributive justice regulates relations between groups and individuals. [And] Social justice refers to the rights and obligations of society and individuals to one another" (*Catholic Encyclopedia*). This, in turn, gives us justice as a moral virtue, or also known as one of the cardinal virtues: "Justice is the moral virtue that consists in the constant and firm will to give their due to God and neighbour. Justice toward God is called the 'virtue of religion.' Justice toward men disposes one to respect the rights of each and to establish in human relationships the harmony that promotes equity with regard to persons and to the common good. The just man, often mentioned in the Sacred Scriptures, is distinguished by habitual right thinking and the uprightness of his conduct toward his neighbour" (*CCC* #1807).

169. *Note*: Saint John uses an interesting term for the Holy Spirit. In his Gospel he calls the Holy Spirit, the παράκλητος (paraklētos/ *par-ak'-lay-tos*). This Greek word is transliterated into English as Paraclete, and is translated as Advocate (Intercessor, Comforter, and Counselor). *Thayer's Greek Dictionary* defines this word as follows: "one who pleads another's cause before a judge, a pleader, counsel for defense, legal assistant, an advocate." Saint John uses this legal judicial term for the Holy Spirit. The Holy Spirit is our Lawyer, pleading our cause before our Judge.

170. *Note*: The Church in Her authority (Mt 16:19), and Her wisdom (Mt 18:15–18) dispenses this form of judgment (1 Cor 5:1–5); however, there is a recognition that any such verdict is ratified in God's sight (1 Cor 5:3–4), and is done in the true sense of *agape* (ἀγάπη) (1 Cor 5:5; also cf. 2 Cor 2:5–11).

171. *Note*: In an initial response to justice (judicial), a friend of mine objected. However, after further reflection she said: "I was wrong . . . you mentioned a mathematical process to justice—I realized I was using the wrong common denominator, which is why it wasn't adding up. I was using mercy as the common denominator, but it's not. Love is. Love can be expressed as mercy or as justice [judicial]. But it's all [rooted] in love, not mercy. God's justice [judicial] in and of itself is not mercy, but it is loving. This is why it seems difficult to separate it from mercy."

172. *Catholic Encyclopedia.*

173. *Note*: By *not* acknowledging this distinction, we not only make mercy cheap, we make God a tyrant. We make Him out to be a bully, Who imposes our free will, and forces His mercy upon us, even if we like it or not!

174. *Note*: Saint Thomas Aquinas states: "God acts mercifully, not indeed by going against His justice, but by doing something more than justice; thus a man who pays another two hundred pieces of money, though owing him only one hundred, does nothing against justice, but acts liberally or mercifully. The case is the same with one who pardons an offence committed against him, for in

remitting it he may be said to bestow a gift. Hence the Apostle calls remission a forgiving: '*Forgive one another, as Christ has forgiven you*' (Eph 4:32). Hence it is clear that mercy does not destroy justice, but in a sense is the fullness thereof. And thus it is said: '*Mercy exalteth itself above judgment*' (Jms 2:13)" (Saint Thomas Aquinas, *Summa Theologica*, pt. I, question 21, article 3).

175. **Note:** "*When Jesus had lifted Himself up, and saw none but the woman, He said to her, Woman, where are these your accusers? Has no man condemned you? She said, No man, Lord . . . Jesus said to her, Neither do I condemn you* [Jn 8:10-11] . . . What then Lord? Do You favour sin? No, surely. Listen to what follows, *Go, and sin no more* . . . For did He favour sin, He would have said, Go, and live as you will: depend on my deliverance: howsoever great your sins be, it matters not: I will deliver you from hell, and its tormentors. But He did not say this" (Saint Augustine, *Commentary on the Gospel of Saint John*).

176. Cardinal Walter Kasper, *Mercy: The Essence of the Gospel and the Key to Christian Life* (New Jersey: Paulist Press, 2013), 53.

177. **Note:** "There are two kinds of presumption. Either man presumes upon his own capacities (hoping to be able to save himself without help from on high), or he presumes upon God's almighty power or His mercy (hoping to obtain His forgiveness without conversion and glory without merit)" (*CCC* #2092).

178. **Note:** Harkening back to the limitless vengeance of Lamech in Genesis 4:24, "seventy-seven times," Jesus, using the exact same words found in the Septuagint, suggest limitless forgiveness, "seventy-seven times." In addition, "seventy-seven times" equaling 490 is considered the year of the Messiah according to the prophecy from the prophet Daniel (Dan 9:1ff).

179. This quote is attributed to Saint Francis de Sales and/or Saint Augustine.

180. **Note:** Interestingly, in this parable when Saint Matthew writes: "But he refused. Instead, he had him put in prison until he paid back the debt" (Mt 18:30). The word he uses for debt, ὀφείλω (opheilō/*of-i'-lo, of-i-leh'-o*) in Greek, is the exact same word Saint Luke uses in the Our Father (the Lord's prayer): "and forgive us our sins for we ourselves forgive everyone in debt [opheilō (ὀφείλω)] to us" (Lk 11:4). In Saint Matthew's own recitation of the Our Father (the Lord 's prayer), he uses two alternative words, which also means the same: "and forgive us our debts [ὀφείλημα (opheilēma/*of-i'-lay-mah*)], as we forgive our debtors [ὀφειλέτης (opheiletēs/*of-i-let'-ace*)]" (Mt 6:12).

181. **Note:** "Resentment and anger, these are foul things too, and a sinner is a master at them both. Whoever exacts vengeance will experience the vengeance of the Lord, who keeps strict account of sin. Pardon your neighbour any wrongs done to you, and when you pray, your sins will be forgiven. If anyone nurses anger against another, can one then demand compassion from the Lord? Showing no

ENDNOTES

pity for someone like oneself, can one then plead for one's own sins? Mere creature of flesh, yet cherishing resentment! Who will forgive one for sinning? Remember the last things, and stop hating, corruption and death, and be faithful to the commandments. Remember the commandments, and do not bear your fellow ill-will, remember the covenant of the Most High, and ignore the offence" (Sirach 27:30-28:7).

182. **Rabbinic Tradition:** Collections of literature and traditions from prominent rabbis just before the time of Jesus, and ending in the first century.

183. **Note:** Do not fool yourself into thinking that you or I are better than a Hitler or an Osama bin Laden. We must recognize within ourselves that we are no better than they are. For under similar circumstances we might not fair any better. Yes, we are also capable of doing the same. It is only through the grace of God that we are not. So, the glory goes to Him and not to us. "For we ourselves were once foolish, disobedient, deluded, slaves to various desires and pleasures, living in malice and envy, hateful ourselves and hating one another. But when the kindness and generous love of God our savior appeared (not because of any righteous deeds we had done but because of His mercy), He saved us through the bath of rebirth and renewal by the Holy Spirit, whom He richly poured out on us through Jesus Christ our savior, so that we might be justified by His grace" (Ti 3:3-6). In addition, in our loftiness we might dare to think that we would stand up to the German Nazi if we were there at that time, but the fact is the vast majority of us would not. We might also dare to think that we would stand up to the chief priests and not scream out "Crucify Him," but again the fact is the majority of us would not.

184. **Note:** With distinctions, there is interplay within these three words. I am presenting it in three steps for ease of understanding. The first step is *Atonement*: to "cover up" or "propitiate" or to make "reparation" or "reconciliation" (*New Catholic Encyclopedia*), or to "wipe clean" or to "appease" or to "purge" (*Mounce's Dictionary*). "Jesus atoned for our faults and made satisfaction for our sins to the Father" (*CCC* #615). "No man, not even the holiest, was ever able to take on himself the sins of all men and offer himself as a sacrifice for all" (*CCC* #616). Only through Jesus, and in Him— through the blood of Jesus on the cross—reparation is made, two parties (God and us) are brought together in reconciliation. Through divine love, we are reconciled with God (cf. 2 Cor 5:18-19 and Rom 3:23-25). "The Christian doctrine that through Christ's passion, death and resurrection, infinite satisfaction is made to God for the sins of humankind. Through this satisfaction, we are reconciled to God. Christ's atonement consists, not primarily in the intensity of the suffering He endured, but in the perfectly obedient and loving acceptance of the Will of the Father which He displayed in embracing this suffering for our sake. Christ's perfect obedience atones for the disobedience of Adam and wins for us the grace of obedient discipleship and divinizing sanctification. Christ is the 'Lamb of God who takes away the sin of

the world' (Jn 1:29), the perfectly innocent Servant Who suffers in the place of the truly guilty (cf. Lk 22:37 and Isa 53)" (*Catholic Encyclopedia*). The second step is *Righteousness*: upon the cross, Jesus pays our debt so that we may be just, right, innocent, pure and holy before God. On the cross, "when Jesus had taken the wine, He said, 'It is finished'" (Jn 19:30). The Greek word used here for "finished" is τελέω (teleō/*tel-eh'-o*), which not only means to end, to complete, to conclude, but also has an inherent meaning that the debt has been discharged, that the debt has been paid, in full! God in His righteousness in and through His Son makes us righteous by paying our debt; thus, completely dealing with the problem of sin. He, the Righteous One, the One who was without sin, takes on our sin and becomes a sin offering so that we may become sinless before God (1 Pt 3:18; also cf. Gal 3:13). Yes, a quality inherent to Him righteousness is imputed to us: "For our sake God made Him to be sin who did not know sin, so that we might become the righteousness of God in Him" (2 Cor 5:21). This is "expressed paradoxically in terms of sharing and exchange of attributes" (*NAB* footnote). In other words, we are made righteous because of Him and only in Him! And the third step is *Justification*: "Because of our sins the Father gave the Lord Jesus up to death, and for our justification, He raised Him up again" (*The Liturgy of the Hours*, New York: Catholic Book Publishing Co., 1975, vol III, 1102). God raises Jesus, so we who "are now justified by His blood, will we be saved through Him" (Rom 5:9; also cf. Rom 4:25). Justification detaches us from sin (*CCC* #1990). It includes the remission of sins (*CCC* #2019), which infuses us with the necessary grace for renewal. "Our justification comes from the grace of God. Grace is *favour*, the *free and undeserved help* that God gives us to respond to His call to become children of God, adoptive sons, partakers of the divine nature and of eternal life" (*CCC* #1996). Now this infusion of grace leads us to a fourth step, which is *Sanctification*: Jesus tells the adulterous women "from now on do not sin any more" (Jn 8:11). "Sanctification is thus nothing other than the perfection of the life of charity. The chief means of sanctification is the infusion of habitual grace which enables us to turn to God in faith, hope and love. The life of grace is continually enhanced in us through our membership in the Mystical Body of Christ and through our sharing in the sacramental grace that is at the very heart of the Church's life . . . We become holy as God is holy so that we can be fit company for Him for all eternity" (*Catholic Encyclopedia*). We are consecrated. We are in the realm of the sacred.

185. **Note**: Righteousness is *imputed* to us; however, we are *infused* with His justifying grace, which leads to *infusion* of sanctification. In his book, *Not By Faith Alone* (Santa Barbara, CA: Queenship Publishing, 1997), Robert A. Sungenis writes: "Christ does not take on the guilt and punishment of the individual; rather, He appeases the Father so that the latter will not bring His judgment upon His disobedient children" (page 413; also cf. page 115). Nevertheless, Sungenis himself goes on to say: "Conversely, Catholic theologian Joseph Fitzmeyer argues that even though the Old Testament imagery speaks to appeasement of anger, this was not Paul's intent, rather,

Fitzmeyer sees *expiation* as the primary effect of Christ's atonement, citing the use of the Greek word ἱλάσκομαι [hilaskomai/*hil-as'-kom-ahee*] in the LXX of God's forgiveness of sins. The problem with expiation, however, is that it can either be strictly defined (i.e., as payment for sins), or loosely defined (e.g., to make amends, pacify, apologize, etc.). Fitzmeyer does not specify which he is using (the Jerome Biblical commentary, op. cit., page 302). In any case, appeasing God's anger against sin and the subsequent forgiveness for those sins that issue forth from their appeasement are certainly overlapping concepts, neither negates the other" (page 684). Which is the stance taken in this study, namely, that it is an *overlapping concept*, thus *neither negates the other*. That said, read carefully what Paul writes to the Romans: "Since all have sinned and are falling short of the honor *and* glory which God bestows *and* receives. [All] are justified *and* made upright *and* in right standing with God, freely and gratuitously by His grace (His unmerited favour and mercy), through the redemption which is [provided] in Christ Jesus. Whom God put forward [before the eyes of all] as a mercy seat *and* propitiation by His blood [the cleansing and life-giving sacrifice of atonement and reconciliation, to be received] through faith. This was to show God's righteousness, because in His divine forbearance He had passed over *and* ignored former sins without punishment" (Rom 3:23-25) (this is the *Amplified Bible* translation; the input is not mine).

186. **Note:** "And where ought Christ to teach, except on the Mount of Olives; on the mount of ointment, on the mount of chrism. For the name Christ is from chrism, chrism being the Greek word for unction. He has anointed us, for wrestling with the devil. They had remarked upon, Him already, as being over lenient. Of Him indeed it had I been prophesied, *Ride on because of the word of truth, of meekness, and of righteousness.* So as a teacher He exhibited truth, as a deliverer meekness, as a judge righteousness. When He spoke, His truth was acknowledged; when against His enemies He used no violence, His meekness was praised. So they raised the scandal on the score of justice For they said among themselves, If He decide to let her go He will not do justice; for the law cannot command what is unjust: *Now Moses in the law commanded as, that such should be stoned:* but to maintain His meekness, which has made Him already so acceptable to the people, He must decide to let her go. Wherefore they demand His opinion: *And what say You?* hoping to find an occasion to accuse Him, as a transgressor of the law: *And this they said tempting Him, that they might have to accuse Him.* But our Lord in His answer both maintained His justice, and departed not from meekness. *Jesus stooped down, and with His finger wrote on the ground.* As if to signify that such persons were to be written in earth, not in heaven, where He told His disciples they should rejoice they were written. Or His bowing His head (to write on the ground), is an expression of humility; the writing on the ground signifying that His law was written on the earth which bore fruit, not on the barren stone, as before. He did not say, Stone her not, lest He should seem to speak contrary to the law. But God forbid that He should say, Stone her; for He came not to destroy that which He found, but to seek that which was lost. What then did He answer? *He that is without sin among you, let him*

ENDNOTES

first cast a stone at her. This is the voice of justice. Let the sinner be punished, but not by sinners; the law carried into effect, but not by transgressors of the law. Having with the weapon of justice smitten them, He deigned not even to look on the fallen, but averted His eyes: *And again He stooped down, and wrote on the ground.* Thus smitten then with the voice of justice, as with a weapon, they examine themselves, find themselves guilty, and one by one retire: *And they, which heard it, went out one by one, beginning at the eldest.* There were left however two, the pitiable, and the pitiful, *And Jesus was left alone, and the woman standing in the midst:* the woman, you may suppose, in great alarm, expecting punishment from one in whom no sin could be found. But He who had repelled her adversaries with there word of justice, lifted on her the eyes of mercy, and asked; *When Jesus had lifted Himself up, and saw none but the woman, He said to her, Woman, where are these your accusers? Has no man condemned you? She said, No man, Lord.* We heard above the voice of justice; let us hear now that of mercy: *Jesus said to her, Neither do I condemn you;* I, who you feared would condemn you, because you found no fault in me. What then Lord? Do You favour sin? No, surely. Listen to what follows, *Go, and sin no more.* So then our Lord condemned sin, but not the sinner. For did He favour sin, He would have said, Go, and live as you will: depend on my deliverance: howsoever great your sins be, it matters not: I will deliver you from hell, and its tormentors. But He did not say this. Let those attend, who love the Lord's mercy, and fear His truth. Truly, *Gracious and Righteous is the Lord*" (Saint Augustine, *Commentary on the Gospel of Saint John*).

187. ***Note:*** To reiterate, upon the cross, "when Jesus had taken the wine, He said, 'It is finished'" (Jn 19:30). The Greek word used here for "finished" is τελέω (teleō/*tel-eh'-o*), which means to end, to complete, to conclude, but also has an inherent meaning that the debt has been discharged, that the debt has been paid, in full! God in His righteousness in and through His Son makes us righteous by paying our debt, completely dealing with the problem of our sins. God does not close His eyes to our sins, no; He clears the debt of our sins, He paid our debt in full "It is teleō (τελέω)" (Jn 19:30).

188. ***Note:*** Some of you might think this is understood; however, just to be clear let me reiterate, this does not mean we condone the sin, the evil act, and it does not mean we have salvific or redemptive powers.

189. *The Liturgy of the Hours* (New York: Catholic Book Publishing Co., 1975), vol III, 547.

190. ***The Papal Bull of Indiction:*** The formal proclamation or announcement of a Jubilee, which is sealed with the Papal Bull.

191. *Bull of Indiction of The Extraordinary Jubilee of Mercy, Misericordiae Vultus*, numbers 1, 2, 3, 4, 12, 13, 14, 20 and 21.

192. *Godhead*: The essential being of God; the Supreme Being; the Holy Trinity of God the Father, Christ the Son, and the Holy Spirit (*Random House* Webster's Dictionary).

193. *Note*: To be clear, we can state that God does love Himself. However, this is not an egocentric selfish idea of love, nor can we acquaint it to the love of self, as understood by humanity, for God is Trinitarian. He Himself is love, and thus He causes all love.

194. *Salvation History*: "Refers to the whole 'economy' of God's action in bringing about the consummation of His plan for the created natural and human orders, as recorded in the Old and New Testaments, and as continuing throughout history until the end of time. God's plan unfolds in stages and through the instrumentality of chosen agents, communities, and institutions. A particular people are set aside as the locus of God's saving actions: the people of Israel and the Church. God chooses and sends those who will accomplish His saving work: Christ, the prophets and Apostles" (*Catholic Encyclopedia*).

195. *Ipsum Esse*: "Latin for 'existence itself,' it is used to describe God as a subsistent Being, i.e., the Being Whose essence is existence and Who is unable not to exist, unlike human beings or lower creatures" (*Catholic Encyclopedia*).

196. *Note*: "Thou dist not create [us] out of any lack but out of the plenitude of thy goodness" (Saint Augustine).

197. *Hell*: "The place, state, or condition prepared for Satan, his subjects and the unrepentant for all eternity. The term corresponds to the Old Testament Sheol or dwelling of the dead. Theologians generally agree that hell is a place of pain and suffering that is derived from alienation from God. The suffering of those in hell is proportionate to the gravity of their sins, and it is without end. This punishment should not be conceived of as a purely psychological pain, for there is an objective aspect and content to it. Just as heaven involves an objective relationship to God and an objective pleasure, so also hell involves an objective condition and an objective punishment and suffering" (*Catholic Encyclopedia*) (cf. *CCC* #1033–1035).

198. *Note*: According to Saint Augustine, "there is only one object that man has any real right to love—namely, God. The right form of love, *cāritās* [a combination of both *agape* (ἀγάπη) and *eros* (ἔρως), or as stated in this study as *agape* (ἀγάπη)], is in essence love of God. It is man's duty to love God 'with all his heart and all his soul and all his mind'" (Anders Nygren, *Agape and Eros*, New York and Evanston: Harper & Row Publishers, 1969, 503).

199. *NRSV* Translation.

200. Teresa of Avila, *Interior Castle: The Classic Text with Spiritual Commentary* (Notre Dame: Ave Maria Press, 2007), 146.

201. Pope Benedict XVI, Encyclical Letter, *Deus Caritas Est* (*God Is Love*), numbers 12, 14, 15, 16, 17, 18 and 19.

Conclusion

202. **Note:** "[When] Christians say the Christ-life is in them, they do not mean simply something mental or moral. When they speak of being "in Christ" or of Christ being "in them," this is not simply a way of saying that they are thinking about Christ or copying Him. They mean that Christ is actually operating through them; that the whole mass of Christians is the physical organism through which Christ acts that we are His fingers and muscles, the cells of His body" (C. S. Lewis, *The Complete C. S. Lewis Signature Classics: Mere Christianity*, New York, N.Y.: Harper One, 2007, 59).

203. **Note:** Saint Bernard of Clairvaux outlines four stages of loving God, he writes: "In the first stage of love, a man loves his own self for the sake of himself. He's fleshly, so he can't have a taste for anything except in relation to himself. But when he sees that he's not able to subsist by himself that God is, so to speak, necessary to him then he begins to inquire about God and begins to love God by faith. Thus in the second stage, he loves God, but he loves him because of his own interest, and not for the sake of God Himself. Nevertheless, after he's begun to worship God for the sake of his own necessity, and to approach Him by meditation, reading, prayer, and obedience, he comes little by little to know God with a certain familiarity. As a result, he begins to find Him sweet and kind. Then, having tasted how sweet the Lord is, he passes to the third stage, when he loves God no longer on account of his own interest, but for the sake of God Himself. Once arrived there, he remains stable. I don't know whether a man is truly able in this life to rise to the fourth stage of love: I mean, when he comes to love himself only for the sake of God. Those who have attempted this (if there are any) may assert it to be attainable. But to me, I confess, it appears impossible. No doubt, however, this perfect love will be attained when the good and faithful servant finally enters the joy of his Lord in heaven, intoxicated with the fullness of the house of God. There, he'll be so exhilarated that he'll be wonderfully forgetful of himself and he'll lose the awareness of what he is. Being absorbed altogether in God, he'll attach himself to God with all his powers, and ever after be one spirit with Him" (Saint Bernard of Clairvaux, Letter XLVI, to Guiges). Taken from, Paul Thigpen, *A Year with the Saints: Daily Mediations with the Holy Ones of God* (Charlotte, North Carolina: Saint Benedict Press, 2013), day 26.

204. *The Liturgy of the Hours* (New York: Catholic Book Publishing Co., 1975), vol VI, 570 and 1558; vol II, 128 (paraphrase of the two closing prayers).

205. Mother Teresa, *A Call To Mercy: Hearts to Love, Hands to Serve* (New York: Crown Publishing Group, 2016), 147.

206. Athanasian Creed (also known as, Trinitarian Creed). This Creed is attributed to Saint Athanasius (295–373 AD), Bishop of Alexandria, and Doctor of the Church.

207. *Note:* Pope Francis is the 266th pope. He is the current pope at the time of writing this book (2015-2020).

208. *Note:* Some may argue that speculative theology is its own category. Nevertheless, for our purposes, these two categories are sufficient (for we may place speculative theology as a sub-category within academic theology).

209. *Note:* Let me clarify the word "foundational." When I use the word foundational, I am not saying that it is introductory. Here is an analogy that might help. All regions of the world have their staple foods. Here in the West we refer to this as meat and potatoes. This we can call our foundational staple diet. It has sustenance; however, we do not feed this to our newborn babies. In a sense, staple foods are not introductory, we do not give them to our babies right away, but we gradually introduce them to these foods. So, I use the term foundational in the same way; it is foundational as in, it is our staple diet. However, the new Christian has to be gradually introduced to it.

210. *Note:* To be clear, this is not *sola scriptura*. As we know, some things written in Scripture are difficult to understand, and thus can be misinterpreted and/or distorted (cf. 2 Pt 3:16). We therefore cannot read Scripture in a vacuum. Sacred Tradition and Sacred Scripture go hand in hand (*CCC* #80–81 and 2 Thes 2:15).

211. The *World Christian Encyclopedia* counted 33,830 Christian denominations as of 2001.

212. Author's translation.

213. Ibid.

214. Ibid.

215. *Note:* The adherence to *Sola Scriptura*—among other issues—faces an inherent contradiction. For nowhere in Scripture does it tell us which books or letters are considered Sacred Scripture. Therefore, we cannot say "Scripture Only" for Scripture does not tell us what Scripture is. It is the Church—through the Holy Spirit—in Her authority that delivers us and tells us what books or letters are to

be considered Scripture (a process that started around 365 A.D., with the Council of Damascus and ended on 393 A.D., with the Council of Hippo). If you would like to read more concerning interpretation of Scripture, I would recommend you read, Vatican II, *Dei Verbum: Dogmatic Constitution on Divine Revelation*, numbers 11 13, and *CCC*, numbers #109 119. In addition, just as the Word made Flesh, is both Divine and Human, the Word of God (i.e., Sacred Scripture) is also both Divine and human.

216. Vatican II, *Dei Verbum: Dogmatic Constitution on Divine Revelation*, number 12.

217. Saint, Pope John Paul II, Apostolic Constitution, *Fidei Depostum*, number 1.

218. *Note:* "Sacred theology relies on the written Word of God, taken together with Sacred Tradition, as on a permanent foundation" (Vatican II, *Dei Verbum: Dogmatic Constitution on Divine Revelation*, number 24).

219. *Note:* Saint Augustine considers the Septuagint to be inspired. In fact, to this day even some Orthodox Christians placed the Septuagint over the Hebrew text. Even though this translation differs in many places with the original Hebrew it is nevertheless considered inspired. One argument is that the seventy Rabbis (by the way, some state seventy-two Rabbis) were inspired while working on the translation. The other argument is that the New Testament writers used the Septuagint over and above the Hebrew text. We see this in many of the quotes within the new Testaments, for they were virtually taken word for word from the Septuagint, and not from the Hebrew. Here is what Saint Augustine has to say concerning the Septuagint: "The authority of the Septuagint is pre-eminent as far as the Old Testament is concerned; for it is reported through all the more learned churches that the seventy translators enjoyed so much of the presence and power of the Holy Spirit in their work of translation, that among that number of men there was but one voice. And if, as is reported, and as many not unworthy of confidence assert, they were separated during the work of translation, each man being in a cell by himself, and yet nothing was found in the manuscript of any one of them that was not found in the same words and in the same order of words in all the rest, who dares put anything in comparison with an authority like this, not to speak of preferring anything to it? And even if they conferred together with the result that a unanimous agreement sprang out of the common labor and judgment of them all; even so, it would not be right or becoming for any one man, whatever his experience, to aspire to correct the unanimous opinion of many venerable and learned men. Wherefore, even if anything is found in the original Hebrew in a different form from that in which these men have expressed it, I think we must give way to the dispensation of Providence, which used these men to bring it about" (Saint Augustine, *On Christian Doctrine*, book 2, chapter 15, number 22).

220. ***Note:*** The only admonitory note to this statement is that of the Gospel of Saint Matthew. For there is an indication that it was originally written in Hebrew (or Aramaic), and then immediately translated into Greek. Most patristic scholars hold this view. Saint Irenaeus (180 A.D.) mentions that Saint Matthew wrote in his own dialect; Origen (244 A.D.) mentions the tradition of Saint Matthew writing in Hebrew; and there are a few others stating such, including Eusebius and Saint Jerome (in the 300's A.D.). Nevertheless, we do not have the Hebrew or Aramaic text, it is therefore generally accepted that the original language of the Gospel of Saint Matthew is Greek.

221. ***Note:*** I would like to outline three options concerning the study of Sacred Scripture. First, and as mentioned, the most beneficial is to study biblical Hebrew and Greek (this might not be practical for most). Second, is to use various Hebrew and Greek study-aids or tools. Third—this being the absolute minimum—is to use multiple translations.

222. See Saint Augustine, *On Christian Doctrine*, book 3, chapter 25, number 35–37.

223. Saint Basil the Great, *On The Holy Spirit*, chapter 1, number 2) (***Note:*** This is a paraphrase of the text).

224. ***Orthopraxy:*** Correctness or orthodoxy of action or practise (*Random* House Webster's Dictionary).

225. ***Note:*** These types of paradoxical statements are not the same as those used by people who say, "The Bible is full of contradictions." This type of "alleged" contradictions, are not what I am addressing here.

226. ***Note:*** Also stated by Hippolytus of Rome: "Virtue occupies the middle position."

227. ***Orthodox:*** An adherence and conforming to established and correct doctrines and Creeds, in totality (*Random House Webster's Dictionary*).

Manufactured by Amazon.ca
Bolton, ON